T0196394

CALLED
TO THE
UTTERMOST

**A Missionary's Story of How to Identify
God's Call and Thrive in the Extreme**

Chara Vovou

*author*HOUSE®

AuthorHouse™
1663 Liberty Drive
Bloomington, IN 47403
www.authorhouse.com
Phone: 1 (800) 839-8640

This work depicts actual and straightforward events in my life. It reflects my present recollection which may differ from that of others. Names of places and characters and other identifying details have been changed to protect the privacy of individuals.

Published by AuthorHouse 07/31/2017

ISBN: 978-1-5462-0176-2 (sc)
ISBN: 978-1-5462-0177-9 (hc)
ISBN: 978-1-5462-0178-6 (e)

Library of Congress Control Number: 2017911656

Print information available on the last page.

Any people depicted in stock imagery provided by Thinkstock are models, and such images are being used for illustrative purposes only. Certain stock imagery © Thinkstock.

This book is printed on acid-free paper.

Contents

Foreword
One

It was my privilege to get to know Chara Vovou when she was my student in the School of Intercultural Studies. I have counted it a joy to continue to be in touch with her over the intervening years.

Chara has led a fascinating life with many turns, detours, and adventures. Some of her adventures have been funny, others sad, and many highly unusual - such as an elephant ride through the jungles of South East Asia. In describing her life, she shares candidly with the reader her defeats, her triumphs, and the lessons she has learned from the Lord along the way.

One of the most valuable lessons she has learned is the importance of listening to God's prompting and responding to His call. She invites readers into her story of finding and walking in God's call. Along the way, she states principles and illustrates them from her life experiences, dealing with issues, such as: How does God equip us and train us for His call? What if we refuse his call? How do we activate our gifts? What if our call requires sacrifice?

In the final chapter she spells out specific steps to know and respond to God's call, by learning to identify gifts, map one's life, and recognize God's timing.

I believe you will find Chara's book enjoyable, informative, and very challenging.

A Beloved Professor
Senior Associate Professor of Language and Culture Learning

Foreword
Two

In her book *Called to the Uttermost,* Chara Vovou tells of her personal journey and the experiences she had in hearing and responding to the call of God on her life.

Everyone's journey is unique and hers is certainly an example of a design with her name on it! God grew her up in the church and her call and response was rooted there. It is amazing to me that with such a background her call was to the uttermost. The stability formed in her family of origin was foundational for her stability in her subsequent response to the call on her life.

I was particularly drawn to the naiveté that is truly an attribute in our own will. It is as though God put it there as a shield of protection. Hallelujah! I noticed that her deception with the marriage was rooted in her desire to be married. Even with all the signs, she conditioned herself not to question. That's what desire does. It blinds us to the surrounding elements and subsequent consequences until they slap us in the face. Again a result of God's impeccable timing. This is a really important point - considering the need for attachment that many women naturally respond to. Contrary to popular opinion, everything natural is not good… She repeated in the book, "He was preparing me and I didn't even know it."

As a woman called by God and a giver, she was on a trajectory of her own choosing. Only when God intervened was the truth revealed, and she was able to stand under the pressure of the mistake and God's forgiveness and continue her response to the call. Chara, having been trained to work hard, perhaps thought that hard work would enable her to overcome the doubt she had in her heart about herself, marriage, her call and her capacity to respond to the call in a way that fulfilled God's vision as it was given to her. View the challenge on your personal call and respond or not by giving and grace.

Her experiences and dialogue about her preparation and the "realness" it engendered are invaluable. The story of the elephant ride was priceless. Her life organization chart, the life mapping suggestion, and her definition of being a missionary "living among the people" is unique, and I am certain she is voicing the heart of God. She was truly called to God's people in the uttermost parts of the earth. I now know that missions are not all other lands literally, but often the mission field is in your own backyard.

Chara and I met at seminary where I served as program director for The African American Church Studies Program. I am enriched as a person, maid servant of God and female pastor to know her and experience up close her gifts, transparency and giving heart.

Her book called me to look through my own "pains" and see them more clearly as window panes to Christ in me the Hope of Glory.

An Esteemed Woman of God and Dear Sister in Christ
Pastor and Entrepreneur

Preface

You've always heard it said, "I don't know why I'm going through this situation at this moment, but I do know that I'm going through it for a reason." Each experience you go through in life is for a higher purpose. Every circumstance is a training ground for greater works in the future. Every situation in your life is a building block toward your potential and to the calling God has upon your life.

Your response during each circumstance and phase of life is critical to the overall success of what God has determined for you. Your response is what establishes the character necessary to handle the ultimate calling on your life.

In order to adequately fulfill the purpose, you must possess the proper training, skills, gifting, abilities, and experience. God's education program doesn't always transpire in a typical university classroom setting. He provides a life course. You don't always know what class you are in, and you may not even realize that you signed up for the class. However, when you look back over your life, you can usually see from where He has brought you and perhaps have a peek into where you may be headed. Usually, you have some idea of the future. God implants a seed of passion, a dream, a hope, something that you "wanna be" or something that He has told you that you would become.

When I look back over my life, I can see a clear drawn out pattern that God began arranging before I was even aware of the assignment He had on my life. The life lessons have not been pretty nor have they been easy. Sometimes, I have had to repeat a course in order to pass the test.

Now as a minister of the Gospel of Jesus Christ, I have had the opportunity to counsel many people in various contexts, denominations, countries, and venues. In order to find their way, they have had to open up dark portions of their life to me and share things perhaps they couldn't or hadn't told anyone else. Many have been wearing masks. They wear one type of mask at home and come out in the public eye wearing a different face. On occasion, it had been appropriate to share my story with them. They were surprised and could not imagine that I was ever the person I described. They couldn't believe that I did those things or had such experiences in my life. I realized that my story helped them to continue their story. It let them know they were not alone and that all of the struggles could be overcome through the grace of our Lord Jesus.

I have recognized that transparency is the key to success in ministry. Transparency is being real. People need real. The Gospel is real. The message is real. It works. Today, people have seen enough of the fake and false. People want to know that you can identify with their struggle. They want to know that you have met challenges in order to lead them. They want to see that there is hope for them because there was hope for you. People need to know that God will meet them where they are, and they don't have to put a $100 on it and buy it. The gift of God is free. Salvation is free. Deliverance is free.

They have heard enough of prosperity preaching and have seen enough preachers who use and abuse them or the Gospel for their personal gain. So many so-called preachers have manipulated and controlled broken vessels that the Gospel message has become the object of mockery. Oftentimes, the messengers of the Gospel have brought shame to the message of the Gospel. People are searching for truth. People watch ministers' lives and determine if what we live aligns with what we preach. Our lives speak.

People need to know that no matter what they have done God still loves them and has a plan and a purpose for their life.

You have real pain for a real purpose!

Your pain and struggle are real and will be used for a purpose when you completely turn your life to Christ. He turns bad situations around and uses them for His glory. God uses the foolish things of the world to confound the wise. He takes nothing and makes something. He takes ordinary and makes extraordinary.

I am going to pull back the curtain and allow you to take a peek through a few of the window "pains" of my house. I will allow you to see the chaos and dirty laundry in my home. I will share with you the details of those patterns that shaped and molded me for the calling God placed on my life. I am saddened to have to change names and places and that I couldn't use the photos I wanted to show you of real life events. However, I pray that you will be able to see into your window "pains" through my real life story.

I am willing to let you look inside my window in hopes that you can receive whatever God has for you. I anticipate that you will see your calling and your purpose with clarity. I pray that you receive your healing. I hope the message of this book gives you permission to open up and free yourself from the chains and bondage that may be holding you back. It is my prayer that you will know you are special, you are set apart, and you are called for such a time as now to be used in the Kingdom of God.

> *Your story will help someone to continue their story.*

Your life will help someone to find his or her life. Your story will help someone to continue their story.

All aspects of your life have significance toward your purpose and help you to identify God's call. That is precisely the point of this book.

1

Hearing the Call

"Chara, go! For this may be your last chance!" I heard this whispered in my left ear, and I recognized it as the unmistakable voice of God. It was Sunday, September 11, 1975, in the late afternoon. I was sixteen years old.

Our regular church service was over, but my dad, the pastor of a church, in Alabama, at that time, had scheduled yet another service. That one was what we called a "singing" in the South. A special group of singers would come to minister in song for the entire service.

The Altar Call

That Sunday was different for me. As a preacher's kid, I was required to go to church every Sunday, every Sunday night, every Wednesday night, and for all other church events that my dad would preach. At the end of every service, we always had what we called an "altar call," a time when the sermon is complete and the preacher asks if anyone wants to repent of his or her sins, join into the family of God, and give his or her life to Christ. My dad would ask people to come forward and pray at the altar. I just wanted to pray right in my seat. I didn't want to go down there in front of everyone. Dad pleaded with everyone in a tone of conviction and power as if it were our very last moment on earth. He reminded the congregation that we had a choice: heaven or hell; and that in an instant, (Dad would snap his finger), we could be taken into death and face eternity! He would explain that eternity is where we would live forever. It is where we would live either in heaven with Jesus Christ or in hell with the devil, burning in fire without even a drop of water to be tasted.

As a child, I was so afraid and felt guilty each time I heard the altar call. I would go to the altar, cry, pray, and beg God to forgive me. I remember I would sometimes be the first one down and the last one to leave. I would cry earnestly because I wanted to do right and live right. I was sincere, but I always felt I was sinning. I was so young. As I think back, I wonder what sin I could have committed at such a young age that would cause me to feel so convicted. I do remember having a sassy mouth and talking back to my mother a lot. I think perhaps I was feeling guilty and convicted over that.

Or—perhaps I wasn't really feeling guilt. I realize now that, even though I was young, God was preparing me to do His work. God was calling me, but I didn't know how to interpret Him. I only interpreted Him as feeling guilt rather than recognizing that He was calling upon my life and pouring His love upon me. Maybe, I was like a small Samuel in 1 Samuel 3 who heard the voice calling him but went to the Priest Eli instead of recognizing it was God.

1 Samuel 3:4-5 (KJV)
⁴That the LORD *called Samuel: and he answered, Here am I.*
⁵And he ran unto Eli, and said, Here am I; for thou calledst me. And he said, I called not; lie down again. And he went and lay down.

Fighting the Call

Most of my life, I felt I didn't fit into a group. I understand better now, but growing up, I didn't know why I was always set apart. I was not a fit in grammar school. I wore long dresses below my knees when everyone else was in mini skirts. When maxi skirts were in style, I still wanted to try out mini skirts. I remember going to school and rolling up my skirt until I made it really short and then unrolling it before I went back home. I wasn't allowed to wear pants, so that prevented me from participating in many sports that others did. I wasn't allowed to go to movies, so dates, activities, and socials were limited primarily to church events — until I began sneaking out.

When I started high school, I began to experiment with the wrong crowd. Peer pressure to go with the crowd was an overwhelming temptation. After all, I was a preacher's kid, and sometimes, I was called names like "Miss Goody Two-Shoes." Whatever *that* meant. I wanted to fit in. I *tried* to fit in. I began by smoking cigarettes, and then cursing became part of my language, so I could be "cool." One evil birthed another and another. I had a car, and I worked at Jack's Hamburgers after school, so I had some money of my own. I believed *I* was all that *I* needed.

Only God's grace saved my life. Grace is the unmerited favor from God. There was nothing I did to earn this favor! His grace is free. Only His grace kept me out of jail, kept me from becoming pregnant, and kept me from sexually transmitted diseases. Only God's grace kept me from harm and dangers when no one knew where I was and I didn't even know whom I was with. He allowed me to go through that only to turn it around for His glory later in my life. I knew God had a purpose on my life.

Going back to my earlier years, I attended junior high, during the time of racial unrest. Martin Luther King marched, and bussing was instituted in the South. I couldn't understand what all the fuss was about. My family always invited black people into our home, and we went to their homes. Mother taught us to love one another and that God loved all people. She never met a stranger. I didn't understand why I was being called a "CRACKER," and black people were called other horrible names. I couldn't understand why our school children were being bussed from our regular school one day to another school far away and then we couldn't get off the bus because of the violence.

Eventually, all of the uptown, well-to-do white people had either moved or enrolled their children in private schools. Meanwhile, the village white, poor kids seemed to have moved out of town or quit school. Whichever way it happened, I was the only white girl at an all black school. I became the brunt of everyone's anger.

One particularly hard day in school, I went out running and crying. My bus driver asked me why I was so troubled, and I shared with him that I had been told by a group of young boys that I was going to be raped if I came back. What I have come to realize is that all of us, regardless of age, ethnicity, color, and creed, are effected by racism, bullying or whatever the evil may be. It hurts everyone.

That night, my bus driver and the bank president knocked on our door. I answered and they asked to speak to my dad. After explaining the day's events, they offered my dad a job as janitor at the Southern Company if he would put me in the private school. Dad was already the pastor of a church and was also a welder at King Pharr, a canning company. He got up at 4:00 in the morning, went to work, came home, prepared his sermons, prayed, and ate dinner. So, if he accepted the offer, he would also go to clean the Southern Company just so I could go to school in a safe environment.

Dad agreed to take the job, and I changed schools. Sometimes, my father looked so tired, and I wanted to say or do something, but what could I say to a father who was just trying to provide for his children and keep them safe?

Dad took a lot of persecution from the church board for taking the job. They didn't like the fact that their pastor was a janitor and even told him he had to wear a white shirt while cleaning the power company in case anyone saw him.

I was so angry with that particular board member. One Wednesday night, at the prayer meeting, Dad went around the room and asked each person if he or she wanted to pray. Everyone probably thought I would just pass on the prayer because I was so young. However, I was hurt, and I loved my daddy and knew the amazing sacrifice he was making for me. I wanted to protect him, and I couldn't. As a humble servant of God, my dad always turned the other cheek. When it was my turn to pray, I prayed in earnest and then said something like, "…and help that lady to see her sins in what she is doing to my daddy and make her stop…" The lady and the rest of the board were present. I think God and the board got the message because it was bold, direct, and to the point. My personality, my hurt, and all that was inside of me came out clear that night. That was the only way I could protect my daddy - by talking to God.

Well, just watch how God works. That job at Southern Company actually became a huge blessing for our family. Dad moved up the ladder to a meter reader position and retired after twenty-three faithful years of never missing a day of work. If he heard a forecast of snow or other bad weather, he would spend the night in his car at the job, so he would be on time. I learned sacrifice, loyalty, and commitment from my dad. Yet, even his sacrifice couldn't carve out a place for me in my new school. I didn't fit in that school and in that group either. Most of the kids were from well-to-do families; I was from the village, and we were poor. When the kids had parties, I wasn't invited. It wasn't as though I could have attended, but the point is that I wasn't asked. I remember the kids talking about the things they were planning for their party, acting as though I was not even present. I think all those circumstances led me to be the rebellious teen I had become by the time I was in high school…before *The Call.*

That Sunday, there was no guilt drawing me towards the altar. I was sixteen years old and truly rebellious. I had tasted all things that I wasn't allowed and probably should not have had. I had been searching for something in all the wrong places and in all the wrong things. I had had a taste of the real world. I no longer lived in the deep country but had been exposed to the city lights of Big City, Alabama.

I had secretly gone to movies without my parents knowing. I had experimented with smoking and alcohol and even with men. For quite some time, every other word from my mouth was a curse word, except when I was around church people or my family. I was done. If Dad made that altar call again, there was no way I would go. I made a determined decision that I'd had enough. I was one hundred percent sure nothing would sway me.

Then, Dad gave the altar call. I was convinced that he wouldn't have one that day because it was a special "singing" service. But, he did. I sat emotionless as I listened to him plead and beg. I was so full of rebellion and feeling no guilt.

Then, I heard the voice in my left ear. The voice, so sweet but mighty and powerful, said, "Chara, *go!* For this may be your last chance!" It didn't take me long to think about it. I had heard *the voice*! I immediately got up and went down. However, that time was different. I knelt down, looked up, and prayed. I can remember it almost word for word to this day.

"God, I don't know if that was you, but I think it was you, and if it *was* you, this is what I have to tell you. I can't live like my mother and daddy. I don't understand that life. I don't understand who You are. I don't know You, but if You ever want me, come and get me." I left the altar without any tears whatsoever. I felt the greatest sense of peace and love overwhelm me. I felt a sense of release and an embrace from heaven. I knew God had spoken. I knew that God had met me where I was.

I sat down on my pew, the third pew from the back on the right-hand side of the church. I had heard God's audible voice, so I opened the Bible to search. It fell open to Acts 1:4 and the words, *"Ye have heard from me,"* jumped from the page, and then, I really knew! I kept reading:

Acts 1: 7-8 (KJV)

"7 And he said unto them, It is not for you to know the times or the seasons, which the Father hath put in his own power.

8 But ye shall receive power, after that the Holy Ghost is come upon you: and ye shall be witnesses unto me both in Jerusalem, and in all Judaea, and in Samaria, and unto the uttermost part of the earth."

I had been called to be a missionary to the uttermost. Excitement came over me! I knew it; I absolutely knew I was called to the uttermost places of the world! That was the part that reached my heart as I read the Scripture. Not the Jerusalem, Judea, Samaria portion, but to the *uttermost*. That was the place that seemed was far away and dangerous, where no one else would go. That was the place for the worst of the worst situations. It was a place where people were forsaken, forgotten, and didn't seem to have a fit in the world. It also seemed like the place people who had lost their hope would go/be. That was the place for me!

Frequently, Dad would have missionaries from various countries come to our church and give reports of their work. They would show their artifacts, and I would get a thrill when I heard their stories. The more dangerous the story, the more excited I would become.

Later, I learned that God puts a passion on the inside of you and that passion leads you to your calling. God had called me, but I was still young. How could that happen? Where *was* the uttermost? Who *was the uttermost?* Why was I called to go? How could this poor preacher's kid ever get there? How could God use me when I had done nothing but run from Him? There were so many unanswered questions running through my mind and my heart. I didn't know the answers, but the one thing I *did* know, with certainty, absolutely beyond a shadow of a doubt, was that I had been called to the uttermost.

When God calls you, He equips you. He trains you and prepares you for His service. Little did I realize that every aspect of my life was training me for special duty. I knew God had a plan for each one of us. Momma and Daddy had always taught me that. Momma would tell me, "Chara, you are special." I have to admit, I didn't feel special, I didn't look special, I didn't act special, but Momma thought I was special. She always seemed to see things beyond the natural realm. I wish she were alive today, so I could ask her more about these things.

I was the only girl in a brood of five children, the second of the bunch. It seemed I had to be the little mommy and that Momma pushed me harder. She saw something that God was doing in me that I couldn't see.

Momma laid the foundation and equipped me for my purpose and my destiny in life. She didn't love me more or less than the others. It wasn't that I was superior or greater than anyone or better than anyone, but she seemed to know I was unique and held a special calling, that I had been set apart to do a specific assignment that was intended just for me. My life would require a specific pathway, much like what Job 23:10 says, *"He knows the way that I take."*

I am sure that each of my siblings interpreted our family life differently. Why? I believe it was because of the difference in the nature of our assignments. If people could realize that, if they could realize what their own roles were, there would be a lot less jealousy and envy. There would be appreciation and support for each other along the journey. We are all different parts to the whole body.

I didn't know it at the time, but being called to the uttermost requires learning from a different set of rules. Later in my life, I was a nurse in the United States Navy, so I like to use military analogies. Nurses, Seals, and Marines are all in the military, but Seal teams have to play by a different set of rules because of the nature of their missions. Marines have to train differently as do nurses because of their assignment, but they are all military. People may be in the same family, but they have different rules because they have different missions in their life.

Growing up, I never realized the training Momma instilled in me. It is only after I wrote a sermon on *Birthing Greatness* that I understood. The example I used was from Samuel. Hannah wanted a son more than anything, but she was barren.

1 Samuel 2:21 (KJV)
*²¹ And the LORD visited Hannah, so that she conceived,
and bare three sons and two daughters. And the child
Samuel grew before the LORD.*

This verse clearly points out that Samuel was different than Hannah's other children. There were other children, but Samuel <u>grew</u> before the Lord. To understand how Samuel was set apart we must see this verse in its context.

In Chapter One, Hannah was one of two wives of Elkanah. She was unable to have children, but Peninnah, the other wife, not only had children but also *"provoked her severely"* (1 Samuel 1:6 NKJV). Peninnah was the antagonist to Hannah. Can't you see the picture? A "I can have a baby and you can't....hahaha...." kind of picture. This situation grieved Hannah's heart (1 Samuel 1: 8), gave her *"bitterness in her soul"* (v.10), and made Hannah pray continuously (v. 10, 12), as she *"wept in anguish"* (v. 10). Hannah prayed for a son and vowed to give her son back to God. God answered her prayer with the birth of Samuel.

Samuel was known in the Bible to be a great man and prophet. The word "grew" in the verse above means to "become great or powerful, to become important, to be magnified."

When you birth extraordinary things, you experience different types of labor pains. These types of births require many tears of anguish of the soul, bitterness, dedication of vows and continuous prayers, which finally cause the birth to come forth in greatness and extraordinary significance.

God *allows* an adversary to come your way to push you to cry and pray. This antagonist helps you dig deep inside of yourself to get to the core of yourself and discover what God wants to birth in you. If you are currently in a "Hannah" situation, thank God for the adversary helping you to birth your baby! If you are destined to be a Samuel and you stand out above others, it is because you were birthed in a different birth canal with a destiny for your life, with a vow upon your life! They can't see or understand your calling. God hasn't talked to them about your calling the way He has talked to you. Don't allow jealousy, misunderstandings, or anything else from others to stop you. You are on a mission. You are on an assignment: isolated, chosen, picked out, separated unto God for a work that only you can do.

Being Equipped for Your Mission: A Lifelong Process

As you look back over your life, I am sure you can find the various ways God prepared you or taught you. You can identify different lessons that led you toward your destiny and purpose. These are the various ways that God has confirmed His calling to you. When you trace the footsteps behind you, it allows you to see the path in front of you more clearly.

As I retraced my story for you, I noticed Mother had seen something different in me from my very early years that helped to shape my future. However, not everyone has a positive foundation. Perhaps, you didn't have a mother or a father to tell you what they saw in you. Perhaps, your parents didn't even see good things in you. Maybe, you were told your life would amount to nothing.

Maybe, they told you they saw something, but there was no way they would be able to afford what it would take to support you.

Every aspect of your life has significance to your purpose. Don't get stuck in what is meant as your lesson. The trial or difficult time is there to teach you an important lesson, so you can use it in your future to help yourself and to help others. If life throws you a curveball, you must find a way to avoid it. Even negative or bad situations can result in positive knowledge and positive outcomes.

Challenges in life press you to reach the purpose that God has planned for you. It requires a press. Apostle Paul wrote in Philippians 3:14 (KJV), *I press toward the mark for the prize of the high calling of God in Christ Jesus."* The high calling requires a press. To get oil from an olive, the olive must be pressed and separated from the other parts of the fruit. The oil represents the anointing or that which is "smeared" upon you as you take your appointed position. The olive must undergo pressure for it to produce its greatest product; otherwise, it is just an olive. Unpressed olives are still useful because they are edible and delicious. However, olive oil has much greater significance. It has much more to offer and many more uses. You must decide if you want to be olive oil or just an olive.

2

My Way

"I am in love, and I am going to get married no matter what you say." These words embodied my feelings at the time. Despite the many warnings, counsels, and signs, I was still living a rebellious life, running from God and religion. I could not and would not understand that stuff. I knew I had a calling, but I didn't want to answer it, not yet. I was simply blinded by Satan as to who God really was and the truth of His love. But God was being patient with me as He continued to chase me with His love.

At age eighteen, I thought I had fallen in love with a thirty-year-old man. I thought I was mature for my age, and in many ways I was. My mother had taught me well. She taught me to cook, clean, and care for my brothers. I even had a job. I thought I was independent, and I always did very well in school. However, I did not know the first thing about choosing a godly husband or making decisions about long-lasting relationships.

I'd graduated from high school and moved into an apartment with a roommate. Michael worked across the street from where I lived. That gave Michael and me ample time to spend together.

For the life of me, I cannot remember how we connected. I guess I blocked that out! Ha. Maybe I was flattered that he was an older man. He certainly showed me a better side of himself than he did later. After a short romance, he proposed to me and promised me the dream marriage that I had always imagined. I just knew he was *the* one: everything I desired all in one package.

When I announced my plans to Momma, I honestly thought she would have a heart attack. She was so emotional that I walked out of the house to try to tune out the words she was saying to me. I wish now I had listened. Yet, I now realize I had lessons to learn, and those lessons would be part of my story, so I could help someone else later in my life.

While I was growing up, Momma told me, "If you make your bed hard, you have to lay in it." That principle is based in the Scripture's teaching that you reap what you sow, whether good or bad. She was right. I did have to lie in it, but I am so grateful for the forgiving power of Jesus Christ and that through His grace and mercy, He could turn a bad thing around and use it for His Glory.

The tension was thick between my parents and me because I was so stubborn and refused to listen to them. I was determined to have my way. Mom and Dad said they would agree to the marriage if we received counseling through one of the pastors they knew and was associated with their denomination. I guess we put on a good show because the pastor agreed we could get married.

Overnight, Mom got busy planning a simple wedding. My friend made the most beautiful wedding cake. Dad would not perform the ceremony, but he agreed to give me away and stood with the pastor. I wore the same dress that I had worn in a beauty contest just before I graduated from high school. Momma called the guests one by one, and although they were all surprised, they showed up. In two days time, it was done. I was married. I had it *my way*; a life-long lesson that I was yet to learn.

Michael bought a Peterbilt truck and was on the road often as an eighteen-wheel truck driver. I was in nursing school. We were quite busy. It all seemed like a wonderful life, and it was going just like I had envisioned. We had a nice apartment, we were both working, and I was in school. We were having fun, going out, having friends over, taking trips, and riding Harley Davidson motorcycles. Michael took up photography and that only added to our fun. What a life! I have to admit I heard conversations that made me curious about what Michael was doing on the road besides delivering goods, and I saw a few signs that let me know something wasn't right, but I wanted to stay in denial. I didn't want to deal with anything unpleasant. And, as long as life was like it was at that time, I thought I could just let things ride.

Keeping the Dream Alive

When I was in the second grade, I was seated in the first row by the window in Mrs. Dorn's class. One day, while looking out the window, I had a daydream. I had just read a book about Clara Barton and another about Florence Nightingale and the Crimean War, and both books had made deep impressions upon me. As I daydreamed, I could see myself gathering wounded soldiers underneath a huge oak tree and nursing them back to health. That dream made me feel like I was doing something good, something I'd really want to do.

I carried that dream with me and constantly told my father about it. I knew he had wanted to be in the Marines, but when he was called to preach at age fifteen, he knew he would not be able to fulfill that dream.

"Dad," I would often ask him, "can you call the military and ask them if I can join?" He knew I was too young, but he encouraged me to keep studying, so one day I really could. When I was in my mid teens, I asked my dad the same question. That time, Dad said, "Call them." I found a recruiter's number, and the recruiting office told me what I had to do in order to join the military as a nurse. That was my plan. Marriage, thank God, did not interfere with that plan.

Becoming a Navy Nurse

I graduated nursing school and told Michael I had always wanted to be a military nurse. Michael was supportive of the idea of me joining the military, so I researched the branches and the requirements. The Navy was the only one, at that time, that would still accept a three-year program diploma in nursing. The others required a Bachelor's of Science degree. I think the requirements have changed now.

My big day finally came. I raised my hand, took my oath, and off to Rhode Island for Officer Indoctrination School I went. Officer "boot camp" — although difficult and challenging with the normal kinds of things you hear about like marching, exercise programs, early wake up calls, etc. Now that I look back, my naivity seems sort of funny.

The only thing I knew about the military was what I had seen on TV. Most of that was silly comedies like "Gomer Pyle" or old war movies my dad would watch. I had no idea what an officer was. I just knew the military had become my momma and my daddy …well, sort of. Our boot camp was made up of professionals: doctors, lawyers, nurses, engineers, and such. We were called the staff officers; our duties were to support the line officers and mission. Our training wasn't as rigorous as the fighters'. We were taught how to eat at the Captain's table, how to assume leadership, how to execute the proper salute, how to march, how to learn officer protocols, and such. However, my mind was still on Gomer Pyle.

Our lieutenant asked who would be the team leader for the week. No one readily volunteered, so I did. The team leader was responsible to make sure everyone was ready to march to class and other leadership duties. Every morning, I knocked on everyone's door to be sure they were awake at least an hour before they even needed to be awake. We slept two to a room rather than in open quarters. I wanted to be sure that we were on time, and I was scared that we would be late. I didn't want to be yelled at by "Sergeant Carter" or our lieutenant. I think that week was the only week that everyone made it on time, and we actually marched without a straggler, but wow did I hear from the troops!

I wondered why my husband didn't come to my graduation, but I chose to believe that it really didn't matter. Rhode Island is a long way from Alabama and maybe we didn't have the money.

Whatever, I thought. After graduation, Michael and I were on our way to California and I started my new career in the United States Navy.

I was processed into the Naval Hospital, and Michael got a job in photography. We were having fun. Fishing, camping, photography shoots, parties, and friends; deep down, I still knew something in our marriage was wrong, but I still didn't want to face it. Michael would stay late at work and take the ladies home. I knew there was more, but I told myself I must have been the problem, and I wasn't perfect either. Besides, if I talked to him about my concerns for us, he would say I was making things up and unjustly accusing him. I could hear my mother say I had to lie in the bed I made, and I sure didn't want her or Daddy to know I had made a mistake. And, to tell the truth, I was still having fun, so I didn't need to face the truth yet. Denial was still okay with me.

3

Join the Navy and See the World!

An overseas duty assignment was coming my way: to the Philippines. It was perfect. Michael could do wedding and portrait photography. We could both go, and he would be self-employed.

The tropics and the Philippines. Life couldn't get any better. I made rank to full lieutenant, and Michael was involved with his photography and meeting many people, especially locals. We spent many hours off base, enjoying

I now realize how that was part of my training for mission: even though I was not thinking about God and His plan for me in those days, He was equipping me even still.

the culture and foods of the wonderful Filipino people. I think I have tried every food, except balut (the rotten egg with the duck embryo inside). I even ate dog meat on three occasions. To follow the customs while I was in the Philippines, I had to eat what was served; otherwise, it would have insulted the cook. I now realize how that was part of my training for mission: even though I was not thinking about God and His plan for me in those days, He was equipping me even still.

As a matter of fact, a tribe called the Negrito lived in the nearby jungle. General Douglas MacArthur had promised that group, known as the original Filipino, a very short black people, free medical care as long as the United States had a military presence there. The Negrito people would come in by the dozens from the jungle, the men wearing just a cloth to cover their front male parts and the women sometimes with their breasts exposed. The close exposure to a different people fascinated me so much. It reminded me of the time Dad had asked the missionaries to come in and bring their artifacts, and there I was so close to the jungle.

The hospital was actually *in* the jungle. Monkeys were everywhere. The Negrito tribe was given such privilege because they helped protect the jungles during the war and kept intruders from entering the base. It was said they used to put the heads of the intruders on stakes as deterrents for the others. Negritios, during my years in the 1980's, still helped to train the military in jungle warfare. They always liked me to be their nurse, and I told them I wanted to meet the king of the tribe. They made arrangements for King Abraham to come and meet me. He invited me to their village. I brought hot dogs, rice, M & M's, marshmallows, and sodas; then, I headed, by foot, into the dense jungle. They carried the supplies on their shoulders, one person in the front and one in the back, using a bamboo stick placed through the ice chest handles.

We walked for hours up and down mountains in the hot and humid weather, with bugs flying all around, as we picked bananas on our way. We arrived at a camp made of small open bamboo huts where we cut the leaves from the banana trees and made tablecloths. We cooked the hotdogs over the open fire, and the Negritos showed me how to cook rice in the bamboo stick. I taught them about M & M's and how to roast marshmallows, which they absolutely loved. At the time, I did not know anything about demons, but they showed me their tribal dances, which would usher in evil spirits. God's protection was upon me. He was training me for the mission field, and I didn't even know it.

"Chara, the Children"

Michael had become very good friends with a local policeman with whom he would go out and get drunk. He grew less interested in my military affairs and refused to come to my galas. I would always be alone at the military balls and other events. People would ask me about Michael, and I would cover for him by saying he was busy or working or offer some other story.

Michael had never drank alcohol in the States. However, he was then drinking heavily. One night, I literally had to pull him up the stairs and put him in a cold bath. As I was pouring cold water on him, he began to cry.

"Chara, the children," he cried. I thought he was talking about the poor children he had seen in the Philippines, and I chalked it all up to the alcohol. Yet, there was something strange about the way he said it. It annoyed my spirit; I felt like there was more he had to say, but I had no other reference, and he was too drunk to continue. Years later, I would find out he had been babbling about his own children: children I knew nothing about, children he had neglected and never supported. Maybe, just maybe, he was experiencing a moment of guilt over his absence in their lives.

Pubic Lice! Really?

As soon as I discovered those nasty little bugs, I took one to the emergency room where I worked and secretly asked the doctor I worked with. He confirmed it. It was lice. And guess where Michael allegedly got it! He said he got it from sitting in a chair that someone else had sat in who must have had lice. Really? I still was not what you'd call a woman of wisdom, but I was not the eighteen-year-old, newly married, bright-eyed child-bride. I was wiser then. However, the game had changed. As I began to question things, *I* was the one who was either blamed, the one who had lost my mind, or the one who was going crazy, and so forth. It was more peaceful not to say too much and to just gather my evidence quietly.

Michael decided he wanted to get a job on base, but I noticed he kept answering that he had never been in the military on the application. He explained to me he had lost his discharge papers and his service member number. Service member numbers were used before social security numbers. Didn't he know that I was *in the military*, and I was aware that you could *request your number from archives*? Something was wrong with his story, but I just filed it in the back of my mind. I didn't realize how God was watching over me until I got back to the States.

I was stationed next in Northern California, and things went from bad to worse. I was in school getting my Bachelor's in nursing, and Michael and I grew further apart. Although still living under the same roof, we eventually went our separate ways. I began to meet other men, and whatever he did was fine with me. As far as our marriage was concerned, I knew it was over, but I still wasn't ready to face the truth. Pride kept me from saying I had made a huge mistake in my life, and I did not want to tell anyone that life at home was absolutely miserable.

Pride Comes before Destruction

Destruction came at the next duty station: Illinois Naval Hospital. With the last vestiges of pride-filled hope, I bought a home and, still in denial, put both our names on the loan. I always wanted to own a home, so I made my dream come true. It included three bedrooms, a basement, a large backyard, a two-car garage, a fireplace and more. Michael worked as a photographer, but my salary in the Navy was what supported us.

During that tour, I was promoted to lieutenant commander (LCDR). Michael had always told me when I made LCDR he would buy me the two-seat, red Mercedes convertible that I dreamed of having. Instead, when I made rank, he just said, "Oh good, more money."

As if that was not enough, I became very sick, and the doctors couldn't figure out what was wrong. My director of nurses thought I was just faking and gave me a rough time.

However, she made my schedule and was ordered by the doctor to put me on light duty. One night, I thought I was dying. My color had changed to grey, and I was bent over in pain. I felt something inside of me rupture. Michael was not at home. I knew the surgeon on call, and I knew enough that I did not want him to touch me in case I needed surgery. I made the decision to stay at home until morning, after the shift changed.

In excruciating pain, alone, and scared, I lay curled up in the fetal position. In the morning, I went to the hospital and had emergency surgery for three ruptured fibroids the size of grapefruits. I was toxic. I was there for seven days, and Michael only visited me the one time when I asked him to bring me some things. Just a week or so after I returned home, snow covered our driveway, and I was forced to shovel the snow without any help from Michael.

At that point, I was ready to let go.

Letting Go

I found a lawyer and asked her to file the paperwork for a divorce and get it over with. As she listened to me, she immediately refused.

"Chara," she said, "something is not right with your marriage. Has he ever been married before?" I knew something was wrong with my marriage. That was the reason I went to her. However, I explained Michael had signed the affidavit when we married stating he had not been married prior. The lawyer insisted that I find out. I married Michael in 1977, and then, almost twelve years later, she wanted me to find out if he'd been previously married!

I was in Illinois, and our marriage took place in Alabama. I had to reach out to Momma, the very person I hurt many years before. But, she was there ready to help me. There is something so special about mothers. They are forgiving and hold out their arms to embrace you even when you have done them wrong. I called her and asked if she could go down to the courthouse to see what she could find.

Momma called me the next day with a house deed that said, "husband and wife," a deed that had Michael's name on it with another woman. I proceeded to look up the woman and found her still with Michael's last name. She said she still loved him, and she would offer me no information regarding their divorce or lack thereof. She then asked me if I knew about Rosa and the kids.

What?! I was angry more than hurt, but I was on a mission, and I had become skilled at putting emotions where they needed to be. She gave me Rosa's phone number, and I called her. She had not heard from Michael since he left without warning, leaving her with the kids. The kids had not seen their dad since they were very young. They were then in their twenties. I invited them to drive from another state. They arrived while I was at work. I was never able to reach Rosa again after that visit. It remains a mystery.

I was getting a good lesson in how to be a "private eye." I drove several hours to Michael's hometown and met with the Veteran's Administration (VA). The VA representative advised me how to search for birth certificates. I obtained birth certificates of his children (court copies), listing his name as the father. The VA told me about Michael's father being in the military, but there was no record of Michael in their system. I was baffled.

Michael told me he'd been a medic and had been shot down

during the Vietnam War. He showed me the scars on his chest and neck. The Veteran's Administration assured me he would be receiving benefits if that were the case, and he would be on file. I called the archived records departments to have his military records sent to court.

Our court proceedings took almost three years. Michael told me he was going to break me financially. He did. Each time he and his lawyer came to court, they would file for a continuance. His lawyer was a reserve military officer, so he got special requests for continuation, and each time they continuued, it drove my lawyer's bill up even the more.

When Michael's military records arrived to the court, it was all we needed. Michael *had* been in the military, but he had robbed a military post office and had been dishonorably discharged. Oh my! Yes, and there *was* another wife. When asked in court a few months earlier if he had a wife, he admitted to having a wife when he was in the military. He explained that his wife was too young, so her father had the marriage annulled, but there it was on his page 2 (the information page of his military record). At the time of their marriage, his wife was 40, and he was either 16 or 17 and told me he had frauduantly enlisted. They had one child. I told the lawyer to ask him to repeat his testimony about his wife's situation and then show him the document. He stuttered and then said, "That is not my signature." The judge looked at the signature and yelled at him.

After fourteen years of what I thought was a marriage, the judge granted me an annulment from the state, retroactive to the date of my marriage. That was very rare! Michael could not produce any divorce papers from any marriage. I was a victim of polygamy and didn't even know. The judge gave me my name back.

Of course, I had to deal with the issue of the house, which became a business arrangement at that point. I had to foreclose on it, but he never got anything, not a penny, out of it. He told me he wanted half of my retirement, but the judge saw through the lies and deceit, and God protected me from a man I never even knew.

The foreclosure still effects my ability to get a full VA loan. We reap what we sow (Galatians 6:7). However, God's grace is sufficient. He sees to it that I have everything I need, and His love is abundant.

Before You Say "I Do"

Do you really know the person you are going to marry? Have you two discussed details of your lives? Where are the gaps? Who is the person? What is the character of the other person? What are his/her values? When I ask these types of questions to people who are considering marriage, the most common answer is that he/she is "nice" or "we share similar interests." It takes more than *nice* to make a marriage work. Are you of different faiths? How will you raise the children together? Does your partner think the same way you do on the subject? Character is deeper. Who is the person? What are his/her values? Do you love family and he/she doesn't. Do you love children and he/she doesn't? Does he/she believe in abortion and you don't? Do you like luxury living and he/she could care less?

These seemingly simple issues can cause D-I-V-O-R-C-E. Don't be so quick to think that this one person is the only one who could fulfill your dreams and your needs. What are your needs? Why will it take a man or woman to fill those needs? Are you content with yourself? What are your issues? Examine those areas first.

Concerning the man, if he is going to be the leader of your family, how is he showing you now that he is a leader? Does he lead you in prayer, even on a date? Does he offer to take you to church rather than a bar? Does he take the lead in serious issues? Does he include you in decision making? How? Does he listen to your voice? Does he have a job? Is he stable in his employment history? Does he show you respect? Does he communicate or ignore you and your desires? Does he blame you rather than work through problems with you?

Regarding the woman, is there something that really irritates you about her? Don't forget to discuss sexual issues. Has she been raped or mistreated and perhaps has no desire for sexual relations. Does she believe sex is for conceiving children only? Does she show you respect? Don't think she will change when you get married. If she shows no sign of being a good wife or good housekeeper now, don't expect that it will change when you marry.

I wish I had asked to see Michael's papers from the military and not taken it for granted the fact that he told me he had been in the military. I wish I had known whether he had really been shot down from a helicopter and hurt during the Vietnam War. I wish I had researched his military history a bit before I said, "I do." I wish I had realized that something was not quite right with an eighteen-year-old marrying a thirty-year-old. I wish I had listened to my parents. I wish that I had learned to ask questions.

I wish I had realized something was missing in me, and I was just trying to fill a void. I wish I'd asked myself all of the questions I asked you in the previous paragraphs.

I was searching for something and falling for anything. I didn't realize I was searching for the Truth, the True One, who could fill my longing and bring me to realize my dream. He was the One who gave me the dream. He was the One who planted the seed in me even before I was in my mother's womb (Jeremiah 1:5). He was the One who knew me, who created me, who formed me and had a plan and purpose for my life (Isaiah 43; Jeremiah 29:11). He was calling me, but I was pushing Him aside and trying to do it my way. His hand was outstretched, but I couldn't see it, for I was blind. I didn't want to see it. I associated Him with rules, church, and a weird lifestyle that I just couldn't get into. I would have to be chased until I could run no more.

> *I was searching for something and falling for anything. I didn't realize I was searching for the Truth, the True One, who could fill my longing and bring me to realize my dream.*

The End of *My Way*

I never did like turbulence. I never liked sitting in a metal shell up in the air having no control, rocking back and forth, up and down, in the sky, leaving my life in the hands of someone I did not know. I had no idea, but I was in for a rocky ride and all control would be stripped from me.

During those miserable days, during divorce proceedings, I met a man on military reserve duty in Illinois. We were golfing and teamed up. He said he saw how I could drive the ball and decided to join me in play. I had learned to play pretty well in the Philippines from Eddie, my caddy, on the military base golf course.

I was safe, I thought, from falling in love. I wasn't ready for a long-term relationship. Stephon lived in New York, and I was in Illinois. It would be a temporary relationship or long distance at best. However, he invited me to New York, and he would visit me wherever I was.

For years, we had a long-distance relationship. I knew he was married, but I also knew he and his wife were not living together and he considered their relationship over, except for his responsibility to his two daughters. I should have been asking questions, but I guess I had not learned from my last experience. Why didn't I ask questions? Was I just afraid to hear the answers? Did I not want to hear the answer? What was the need in me that was void and empty that caused me to fill it with false hope? I should have made myself make some tough decisions and face reality, but my emotions overtook my ability to reason appropriately.

Stephon had a high level position in state government. He was also in the military reserve, so I felt he understood and appreciated my career. The three long years of court were over for me when I came to my last duty station in Florida. I had no intention of retiring when I got there, but circumstances led me that way. Stephon and the realtor helped me buy a house. Life was good.

Finances were tough due to the bills I had been left with from the marriage, but I managed. I was free, and Stephon was an awesome man. I was growing to know him and love him. I finally met his mother and family, and Stephon promised me that we would have a life together. We dreamed together about how that looked.

He visited me almost every other weekend. Sometimes, he stayed for a week or at least three days. Other times, I would go to New York. Christmas in the city was great. Snow covered the city, chestnuts roasted on the kiosks' open fire, and ice-skating at Rockefeller Center with the huge Christmas tree was delightful.

As the years passed, I wondered how we would have a life together if Stephon did not get a divorce. When I would try to discuss it, I was told it was not a subject to discuss. I had been down that road before. It sounded familiar. I couldn't believe how wonderful our relationship was when we couldn't discuss his marriage. Everyone that knew us admired Stephon and knew we were meant to be together. One day the phone rang as we were sitting at the breakfast bar in my home. It was Stephon's mother calling to tell him his wife had just died. He had to leave immediately.

I was promoted to commander, and I retired in 1998. President Clinton asked for the high ranks to retire early under a program called TERA (Temporary Early Retirement Act). It seemed a perfect fit for me at the time. I had no idea it was God preparing me for my destiny, which was about to come into view. Stephon and I discussed how I should I introduce him during my retirement speech. We agreed that fiancé was appropriate. I was leaving Pensacola to live with him in New Jersey. I would leave the house in Florida, and we would use it as a summer home.

That was when I realized that Stephon had not prepared his daughters for my arrival the way I thought he said. I lived with him and his daughter for three years until I acknowledged that living there wasn't a fit for me. I loved this man with my whole heart. We had been together for almost twelve years, but I couldn't live under the same roof given the circumstances. I am sure the death of their mother and their dad living with another woman caused much of their animosity toward me. Stephon and I were still together, but I simply couldn't live there.

I moved to New York on 9th and 34th Street and got a director appointment by the governor of New York state. The position had not been filled for some years. A few temporary directors had been assigned to the position, but the department was in total chaos when I assumed the position. The staff had worked under marginal guidance; state surveys were months and even some years behind, staffing issues had not been adequately dealt with, and the problems kept coming. The staff constantly ran to the union representative complaining about the new way of work. I created a schedule that would catch us up on the surveys within the year. Instead of one survey a week for the whole office to complete we could do two or three. I thought it was very reasonable for an entire staff. The schedule could be seen online by the chain of command. That overwhelmed the staff. However, the "bosses" loved it.

Then, politics came into play. It was time for re-election, and the Union made an issue of the low morale of the staff, stating that the governor might not get re-elected if the staff grew too unhappy. I *was* apppointed by the governor. Lies, games, and deceit filled the office. The boss supported whoever was the last person in her office. She would order me to make a change and when the change was done, the staff complained to her. I would be called on the carpet for making the change she ordered me to make, as she completely denied having made any such order. That became the pattern of the day in the midst of confusion and chaos. One day, I was given a breathtaking letter of recognition for bringing the department into compliance, and a few days shortly after, I was asked to turn in my resignation.

I was absolutely floored. Finally, I had arrived. I had my ideal second career, appointed by the governor. I made a great salary and still had my retirement. I was into the six figures then. New York – there I was - high heels, fashions suits, big office on 34th street, and it was all gone in one moment. I was devastated.

Stephon didn't seem to have empathy. He couldn't understand how I could lose the director level position. He tried to give some words of comfort, but the next day, he told the real truth as to why he couldn't console me.

The next day Stephon called to say he was coming over. He sat in my studio apartment. I was on the futon, and he sat in the chair next to my desk. He grabbed my hand and said, "I have to stop pretending. I don't love you anymore."

Pretending! I could not believe what I just heard.

I was forty-three years old with no idea what I was going to do. Who would hire me now? How could I live without Stephon? That void was so incredibly empty. I didn't have the motivation to work because I was still too devastated, depressed, hurt, and vulnerable. I was still trying to process these major life-changing events.

Fourteen years with a husband that wasn't my husband and twelve years with a man who promised me the life of my dreams. I had recently spent all my money on getting an apartment in New York, I had lost my job the day before, and the man I absolutely loved just told me he was pretending to love me.

My world sank. My tears were uncontrollable. I couldn't believe what I had just heard. Really! I tried to look back and find the warning signs. I had seen them clearly with Michael. I seemed to recall a few with Stephon, mostly because he would never commit to marriage. I seemed to make excuses for him about that. I lived with him. He put me on his death insurance. It was like we were married. Right?

Don't Rush God

Marriage is a holy sacrament. God designed it. He designed it to be a covenant between a man and a woman. God has to be the center of the covenant. A covenant is more than an agreement or a contract. God gave a covenant to us, and we are required to abide and keep the covenant when we accept Him as our Lord. However, we cannot keep the covenant without His help. Our humanness gets involved. We need God to help us when our human side wants to quit or wants to go with our feelings. A marriage cannot stand without God. God has to put the marriage together. When people choose mates on their own without God's direction and approval, it is headed, at some point, for disaster.

I cringe most often when I hear someone say they are going to get married.

Once a young minister wanted me to pray for him concerning someone he was thinking of entering into a deeper relationship with and possibly even considering marriage. He sent me a picture of her and asked me what I saw. I told him I saw claws in her eyes. He was absolutely floored.

He began to tell me of her past. Her past was actually who she had become then. Her past was horrific, and she had not dealt with the pain and had gone from relationship to relationship. He told me how they could work it out, how she was saved, had so many gifts, and on and on. By the time he finished talking, he could see the claws and could see where his ministry would be hindered.

It was only a month later when the same minister called and wanted me to see a picture of another woman. I stopped him right there. "If you have to ask me if this is the woman for you, then I can tell you it is not. If God hasn't shown you beyond a reasonable doubt that this is the woman for you, then you need to run!" God will make it very clear who is for you. He has a mate for you. Don't be in a hurry. Don't rush God. Don't let your hormones or outside appearances guide you. Let God choose who is the right mate for you. I lost twenty-six years with two men. You may have to wait a while, but it will be worth the wait.

At Death's Door

Before Stephon, I never cried. I was a commander in the United States Navy, and I had four brothers who wrestled me. I prided myself that I didn't cry. My oldest brother used to try to make me cry. He pushed the bone under my nose so hard and tried to bring me to tears. If you don't think *that* hurts, you get someone to do it to you. He tried to make me say "uncle" and quit, but I wasn't a quitter. He couldn't make me. I fought back!

That time was different. Tears rolled down my cheeks from the depths of my belly. They must have been stored for years. I cried for at least ten hours a day for a month. I couldn't stop. I was extremely broken. I wanted to die - literally! Living in the city of New York, I knew the traffic could kill me. In New York, no one even pulled over for an ambulance or police car. I walked in front of cars and taxicabs on 8th and 34th street and tried to get hit as they scurried by and swerved to miss me. How could they miss me? They would usually just blow the horn and expect me to move as they shot me a bird or yelled obscenities to me.

Suicide by traffic didn't work, so I found some pills in the cabinet left over from a past illness. I took them, but they only made me feel sicker. I vomited, but I couldn't die. I wasn't brave enough to cut myself or shoot my brains out. I knew I was in deep depression, but no one knew except me. I didn't seek help nor did I call anyone. I didn't tell anyone at that point Stephon had left me or that I had lost my job and had no money. I just cried. The pain hurt so badly, and I felt hopeless. I was alone in a New York studio apartment in the center of where it all happens. It is certainly where it happened for me.

God Spoke through a Fortuneteller

As a nurse, I knew if I didn't go outside I would truly lose my mind. I went for a walk and the tears continued to flow uncontrollably. No one seemed to care in our big city. It was everyone for himself. I looked up and asked, "New York, where are your bright lights now?" Then, as I was coming up 32nd street, I heard that voice again; the one I had heard when I was sixteen.

"Chara, it's me. I'm back." I recognized the voice.

"Oh no," I responded, "I can't do that."

I continued my walk to a pub across the street from my studio. I drank several glasses of wine, until I could handle the pain, and then, I strolled home. Funny how alcohol never relieved my problem. It gave me a few minutes of not caring, but the problem was still there. I flipped my TV on to have some company, and a loud white lady was preaching, and I caught one word before I changed the channel. "Destiny!" Paula White had spoken one word that penetrated my heart. My destiny. What was it?

I knew of an astrologer, an Indian man in Queens, who read the stars. He could tell me my destiny. He was supposed to the best in Queens. I was determined to go there the next day to find out just what was my destiny. I dragged myself to the subway and found the astrologer. I entered a small one room office with just enough space for his desk and the two of us to sit. His computer was on top of the desk. He showed me some of my stars and made some comments about them. Then, he looked up at me and said in his Indian accent, "I think you need to go to church."

I looked up and said, "God, are you chasing me? I can't hide from you. I can't escape from your presence" (Psalms 139:7). I wondered if God was speaking through the voice of an Indian astrologer, like when He spoke through a donkey in the Bible (Numbers 22). I knew He could speak through who and what He wanted to. He was and always will be God. He had a purpose and a plan for my life, and He was chasing me in order to get my attention. The time and the season was at that moment. There was no way I could escape. I was at rock bottom, and God was chasing me. I had been caught.

> *He had a purpose and a plan for my life, and He was chasing me in order to get my attention.*

I wasn't looking for God. I still didn't want God. But God wanted me. I was reminded of that moment when I was sixteen, and I told Him if He ever wanted me to come and get me. He did.

> *I wasn't looking for God. I still didn't want God. But God wanted me.*

Answering the Call

Faith had been inviting me to church for quite some time. She and I were good friends. We had met at the State Department and have remained good friends even until today. I refused her invitations, always saying I was busy. She knew the deal. She had seen my life and knew from whom I was running. After my experience with the astrologer, I decided the next Sunday I would go to her church.

It was winter of November 2002. I pressed my way to Faith's church in the Bronx, only to find out that they were not having a full service but were going to another church in Uptown New

York. She had plans to go Christmas shopping after church was over, but I was disappointed because I made it that far, and I wanted to hear the message. She changed her plans and went to church. The music was awesome. Jacob, their long time organist, was playing and making that organ talk! I was thinking that was a place I could go back to, and at that exact moment, Faith looked at me and said, "I think you'll come back here."

> *God knows how to meet you where you are.*

I not only went back, but I went to almost every service. However, I still wasn't ready to say the prayer and go through the altar call and fully commit to something I didn't understand. I just sat in the pew, listened, and cried through most of the services. I was too broken. *God knows how to meet you where you are.*

The Meeting Place

It was a Wednesday night, and Ms. Green, a church usher, wanted me to walk with her to the subway. She was an elderly lady, but I was a white girl in Harlem. I was aware of the fact that it was night, so I made the excuse that I had planned to speak to the pastor though I had not planned to do so. Ms. Green yelled across the church, "Pastor, Chara wants to talk with you." Ms. Green, God rest her soul, for she has now gone to heaven. That night I gave my life to Jesus Christ. I didn't really know what I had just done. I just agreed to the plan God had for me, and I asked Him into my heart. I asked Him to forgive my sins, and

I acknowledged that He is Lord and Savior and that He could use me however He wanted to.

Isn't it funny how God uses our ignorance to get a "Yes" out of us? I told Him I was broken, and I had made a mess of my life and wondered if He would fix it. I gave Him permission to do just that. Minister (now ordained Reverend) Brown was assigned to watch over me. She called me at least once a week and prayed with me, ministered to me, guided me, and spoke into my life. I will forever be grateful for her ministry to me.

One day, I was driving and the emotional pain was so great that I didn't know how to deal with it. I was crying from the depths of my soul. I was just driving along the river in Uptown New York. The Lord whispered to me at that moment. "Memorize a Scripture. Repeat it over and over until the pain subsides." The essence of the Lord was so sweet that I could not ignore Him. I often use this concept when I counsel others. The Word of God is sharper than a two-edged sword. It can cut right through the pain.

Supernatural

The pastor kept telling me he saw something in me. He kept telling me God was going to use me. I heard him, but I had no way of knowing what and how it was going to happen. I remembered what Momma said. I remembered my call in 1975, yet I remained clueless. I couldn't get over the fact that I was simply broken and had lost everything.

Minister Brown taught me about fasting. I began to fast and pray regularly. I needed help and help right then! I was taught that fasting was a form of consecrating to God: giving up meals, substituting them with prayer and profound devotion. It sort of says, "Lord, I'm starving for You!" It is the idea of wanting more or growing closer or nearer to God. It is a way to tune out the world and enter into deep communion and meditation with God. The phone, computer, and TV are turned off as much as possible. Some people go to a mountain place or an ocean to be surrounded by nature and to be alone with God.

That particular seven-day fast was significant for me. I read Psalms 119 seven times every day of the fast. It is the longest chapter in the Bible and speaks of longing to know Him, His Word, His statutes, and His laws. I was lying on the futon listening to music about the Holy Spirit, and I noticed my body became completely at rest and was immovable. I was at peace but could not move. I went into a sweet place of awareness. I can

No language contains words that can fully describe His presence.

only describe it to say it was like I was in a place of light, peace, and comfort. I asked God what was happening and if it was Him. I didn't want anything that was not from God. He whispered, "It's me. You are okay, I am giving you an anointing." I didn't even know what an anointing was until later. No language contains words that can fully describe His presence.

After that, I began to have dreams, some in my sleep and some while I was awake, like visions. I began to feel the wind of the presence of the Holy Spirit blow across my face when I would pray, and I began to hear His voice. It was not usually an audible voice but that still small voice whispering into my spirit. God began to reveal Himself in many ways. For the first time in my life, I realized that God had a great sense of humor! I understood that I was in relationship with God. I finally understood that it was more than a man made religion. It wasn't a denomination. It was personal relationship between my Lord Jesus and me. I sensed His love and couldn't imagine why I didn't accept Him before.

One early morning, I was awakened from my sleep. The Holy Spirit said, "Read Ezra 5." It was loud and clear at five am! I said, "Lord, Do you know it is five am? Is there even such a name in the Bible as Ezra?" I was ignorant of the Bible. I had been to church all of my life but really had no idea of the great truths. I knew Jesus loved me and died for me. I knew we were to honor our parents, and I knew about heaven and hell, but beyond that I don't think I paid attention. I didn't remember Abraham or Moses and certainly not Ezra! And definitely not at five in the morning! I was obedient and then went back to bed. The message was about rebuilding the temple. I think God was letting me know He was rebuilding me as my body is a temple for the Lord (1 Corinthians 6:19).

I had a dream. It was a ribbon floating in the air with the word "Preach" written on it. I could hear the word "Preach" in my dream. I awoke telling God that I didn't know the first thing about the Bible. He must be mistaken. I was too old. I already had a master's degree, and I really didn't think I could go to school to learn how to preach with my current income. For the next week, every Scripture I read said, "Preach." It didn't matter where I looked in the Bible. Even if I tried to escape and go to a familiar Scripture that I knew didn't have that word, my Bible would find its way to a verse with the word "Preach" in it. How in the world would I be able to preach!

4

In the Nick of Tithe

My house in Florida finally sold, and I thought I would use the money to pay a few bills. God had a different idea. I paid my tithes, and I felt as proud as a peacock, but something kept nudging me. By that time, I knew what it was. I had learned to recognize the unction of the Holy Spirit. I called and asked my father if I was to pay the tithes on the amount I sold the house for or the amount I cleared. He was treading lightly, but mentioned that I had not paid my tithes for many years. He also mentioned that we could not outgive God. His words took away my justification for saying God would understand and not want me to be broke. I was seeing Daddy's love as he was also trying to teach me. Nonetheless, I couldn't sleep. God kept me awake and gave me step-by-step instructions. I had paid my tithes to my church in New York, so where should the rest of the money go?

I was reading the Scripture, and every verse talked about *thy Father's House* in some form or another. God instructed me to send the money to my dad's church in California. I wrote the check and put it in an envelope; it was then three am. I made the decision to mail it when I woke up later. God was specific. He said, "Now." It was cold and snowing outside, and I had to walk a few blocks to the New York main post office, which was open twenty-four hours. But God wanted me to "overnight" it. I was obedient. I knew nothing of the financial situation regarding my father's church where my brother was the assistant pastor. Upon receipt of the money, my brother called and said the money came just an hour before they had to pay an outstanding bill, and they had insufficient funds. The consequences would have been devastating for the church if they had not paid the bill. The amount the Lord directed me to send was the exact amount they needed!

Faith Impartation

My money was gone, and I had sixty-six dollars left in the bank. I didn't know how I could survive. The phone rang, and it was a Korean neighbor I had met just the month before. Her brain cancer was in remission, and she had just gotten out of the hospital. We spent time together every day praying and going on picnics. She made kim-chi (sour, spicy cabbage) and bulgogi (Korean marinated beef slices). We would go by the river and eat. Each morning, she would call at 9:00 am and tell me to come for breakfast. She would make kim-chi pancakes, kim-chi and eggs, or kim-chi soup. That morning, she said we were going to the mountain. Where was the mountain? I barely knew her enough to spend any place with her overnight, but she insisted.

"God does miracle in mountain." She said, "Me no car; you

no money; you drive; I pay." Then, she taught me about a Korean prayer mountain, a place of consecration to pray and fast.

That night on July 3, 2003 at 11 pm, I cried out to the Lord from a huge rock in the woods.

"Lord," I cried, "I have sixty-six dollars, and you have to answer me tonight. What do I do?"

We went inside our cabin. It was about two am when Mrs. Gah and I finished talking and had turned off the lights. I heard the *voice*, "Move to California." I laughed.

"Lord," I answered, "Did you hear me? I said I have sixty-six dollars. Just how will I get there?" Then I turned to Mrs. Gah and said, "Mrs. Gah, the Lord just told me to move to California."

"You no money; me no car," she immediately replied. "You drive; I pay." I pondered what I would do with the new, chic, and expensive furniture in my New York studio. Then, I heard the Lord direct me to give everything that I owned away, except what would fit in one of my cars. He specifically told me give it away and not to sell it.

One week later, I had not only given away my new furniture in New York, I had given away one of two of my cars. I had just paid over $10,000 for that furniture. We packed and were on our way to California. We had to stop in Florida for the Lord told me to give away *everything* I owned. My things in Pensacola were in storage, and the Lord showed me that I was to give them to a pastor whose wife died because he was raising several foster children. That was the same family I had anonymously sponsored for karate while I was stationed in Florida.

What a shock! Leaving all to gain, as Apostle Paul had written in Philippians 3:8 and going to an unknown land like Abraham (Genesis 12). I had told the Lord before that I didn't know who these guys were, but I had begun to feel I was being taught who they were as I lived out a small piece of their journey in modern times. The Bible was literally coming to life for me. I was beginning to understand its significance, meaning, and application. The Holy Spirit was teaching me.

We were on our way to California and taking our time while driving across the states. We finally arrived on the West Coast at the end of July 2003. I woke that next morning to find that Mrs. Gah had taken an early walk. When she came back she laughed and said she had fallen. At the time, I didn't realize the true impact of her statement. She asked me to take her to get acupuncture, so I searched for a nearby office. When we arrived, she told the doctor to give me acupuncture instead.

"Mrs. Gah," I said, "you wanted acupuncture, not me." She insisted that I get the acupuncture, so we proceeded as she waited in the other room. Upon completion of the therapy, Mrs. Gah went to the front desk, paid the bill, and fell over into my arms. I could barely manage to get her into my car and to a nearby hospital.

Her temperature was raging hot. The emergency room staff began working on her immediately and testing her. The brain cancer had returned, and the tumors had grown dramatically. She woke up in the emergency room for one moment.

I said, "Mrs. Gah, it doesn't look good. Your tumor is back. Are you afraid?" She replied, "No, Chara, faith, Jesus!" Then, she drifted back into an unconscious state.

My first two weeks in California were spent sitting by the side of Mrs. Gah until her daughter could arrive from New York. Her daughter was pregnant and had been advised by her doctor not to fly, so she took the train. Just a week after her daughter arrived, Mrs. Gah died.

After her death, I realized her gift of faith had been imparted unto me.

5

Dad's Work Ethic Instilled

Where do I go from here? My brother had invited me to come to California and live in his apartment complex with Mom and Dad. Years before, he had brought Mom and Dad from Alabama when Mom was scheduled to have open-heart surgery. Four of her five children lived in California, so Mom and Dad sold their home and moved there. Because I had lost everything I owned and God was calling me to ministry, my brother offered me a place to live until I could get further direction. I was getting a little pension from the military but hardly enough to buy a home or even to pay rent. Unemployment from a part-time job was running out, and I was at a complete loss as to how I would live. I had never been in that situation before.

I always had a stable job. As a matter of fact, I had worked since I was ten years old, baby-sitting and cleaning houses for people. I never knew what it meant to not be employed. I shared that characteristic with my dad, I think. He valued a high work ethic and instilled it in me. He always told me, "Whatever you do, be the best."

One day, when I was fourteen years old, we were waiting for Mom to finish shopping at Kmart. "Go over there to Jack's Hamburgers," Dad said, "and apply for a job." I got the job! I got my work permit and began selling hamburgers. I made it my secret goal to be the highest salesperson when they counted my register. I usually was. I pushed those fries or drinks telling everyone why they needed it with the hamburger. The hamburger couldn't be sold alone!

What I really wanted to do was to be a nurse. So when I was just sixteen, I went inside a nursing home and asked for an application. I was told the director of nursing would talk with me and to have a seat. I sat for a couple of hours and finally asked how long I would need to wait. The director finally came out and said she didn't know I was still there. I wore my black velvet dress with a pink stripe at the hem of the dress. I dressed for that interview. I was determined. The director interviewed me.

"Chara," she said, "I hear you want to be a nurse's aide, but you are too young, even with a permit."

I replied, "Even for someone who wants to be a nurse *really bad*?" She paused and then said she would call me. She called me the next day, and I got the job!

I have always worked, so *not* working was a huge adjustment for me. I was in California, and the Lord called me to preach, but I had no idea how to do that. The only thing I knew to do was to find a job and apply for a school to teach me. I really did not want to go back to school and frankly had no money to afford it without a job. I had a diploma in nursing, a B. S. in nursing, and a Masters in management. More school was not on my agenda, but I guess it was on God's agenda!

I knew I needed a job to go to school, so I submitted my application everywhere. I was highly qualified, but job offers were not coming my way. Usually, I could get a job almost instantly. Finally, I applied and was told at my first interview that I was hired as the director of admissions. I was asked to return for a second meeting to greet the managers. Driving to the meeting, I cried and prayed loudly in my car.

"Lord," I said, "You have called me to preach and to go to school. I don't know how to do this unless I have a job. If I have a job, how do I manage the requirements of the intense program of study? I don't know what to do. What I do know is they have offered me a job, and I am going to take this job unless you step in. I don't see any way to turn it down. Only you can stop it, and I don't see how you can at this point because they have made me an offer." I poured out my heart wanting to make the right decision, but felt that was the only decision I could make.

I arrived at the hospital where I would be the new director of the admissions department. I announced I was there for the meeting. It was the strangest moment. The manager got on the phone and began to call everyone because no one showed for the meeting. At that moment, they were too busy to make it. The manager tried to make excuses and apologized over and over. She said she would be in contact with me. Over the next few weeks, there was so much confusion, and I knew God had intervened. He spoke to me, "Chara, from this point on, you work for me and no one else. You must trust me. I am your provider." Well, that was scary for a fairly new believer, but I was a believer. What God says, I believe! I had faith!

Seminary

I searched online for schools. I had no idea what I was doing. I didn't know the difference between a Bible college and a seminary. I began to look for both. I looked at my dad's denomination, because he wanted me look at his alma mater. I knew in my heart I needed diversity. I don't know exactly why diversity was a driving force for me, but I believe God was directing me. I researched the staff of professors at various schools and found them to be white men around age 60. Those were not the schools for me. I needed a more diverse education. I continued to search and asked many questions. What was the difference of Bible college and seminary? One school gave me an answer I could understand. Seminary required a Bachelor's degree and Bible college didn't. I already had a Master's. However, I didn't have any Bible classes. They said that didn't matter.

As I searched further, I read a profound article by the president of the Hardwork Seminary in CA. I didn't know of Hardwork Seminary. I had been "churched" as a child, but I had left the church and had no clue about all the various radio programs, famous preachers, doctrines, big churches, and so forth. I just knew Jesus saved me and that I was in a great relationship with a wonderful friend who talked with me and guided me. I loved it!

The president's article was on diversity! I looked at the staff of professors, and I found they were from everywhere with various backgrounds. When I looked again at my dad's school and saw one of the professors at that school had actually graduated from Hardwork, I talked to my dad, and he validated the school's reputation and history. He said Hardwork was a good school and it had been started by Charles Hardwork who had a well-known radio program. That confirmed my choice, and I felt a little more confident in the direction God was leading me. I called the school, and it just so happened Hardwork Seminary was sponsoring lunch and tours of the school for potential students the very next day. After my tour, I completed the application and was very quickly approved. When God opens a door for you, no one can close it (Revelation 3:8).

Moving back in with my parents was huge for me. I had been married, been a commander in the military, lived on my own since I was eighteen, and at forty-four years old was at home under the roof of my parents. They didn't treat me like a child, but I felt like I had returned to my childhood. I reminded myself of the Scripture about being born again in the Book of John Chapter Three. I literally felt I had to be born again and go back through all the years I had missed at home; I had to go and live at home with my parents, go back to college while under their roof, and then leave again.

My brother began to charge me $500 for rent per month. I saw no way I could continue to pay even that small amount of rent and go to school on my little income. I was able to get loans for my school, but my expenses and debt from my past were eating all of my retirement check. I had almost no money, except for gas and food, and sometimes that was a *by-faith* situation.

My classes began at one of the satellite campus sites. However, in order to graduate I had to take several courses on the main campus. I had to find a place to stay for the summer and take as many courses as possible during that time to make it worthwhile. I signed up for five courses. One of the students was leaving for the summer and wanted me to stay in her apartment. She only charged me a small fee. God worked it out! Little did I know what He was going to do.

I was working steadily, pushing hard to get the courses completed in the short time I was there. I was on my fourth class and became very frustrated spiritually with one of the professor's comments and ways. I talked about it rather strongly to another student when another peer came and listened in. Without any knowledge of my background or anything about me, she said, "You are in the wrong program. You need to be in the missions program."

I was in the Masters of Divinity program. She said for me to follow her to the office, and I could talk with them and decide for myself. I already knew I was called to be a missionary, but I was placed in the Masters of Divinity program for preaching. At the end of hours of discussion, I was reassigned for a dual degree in Master of Theology and Master of Cross Cultural Studies (missions). That allowed me to take the classes I wanted in Hebrew and Greek. The classes I had already taken in the Masters of Divinity would transfer easily. Talk about a faith walk.

The only problem then was all mission and theology courses had to be taken on the main campus two hours north. I had no money for my own apartment and had only one week left. If I didn't take my fifth course I was told I could be reimbursed, check in hand, within hours. The housing office had a listing of apartments available for students. My next three hours were a whirlwind. I had, by faith, changed my program of study, believing God would bring it to pass. I called every number on the housing list. Either no one would answer, the apartment wasn't available, or it was out of my financial reach - until the last number on the list, when a Chinese lady answered. She had a room. Her husband had attended Hardwork thirty years before, and they wanted to give back to the community. They had just bought an apartment complex and had turned one of the apartments into dormitory style living quarters affordable for Hardwork students. She invited me to come and look at the room. A shared room was $250. I picked up my check from Hardwork Seminary, and I went immediately to the apartment. It was situated in a gang and drug-infested area of town, but I took it. In a matter of three hours, God had moved for me. So, I just had to go home to gather my clothes.

A Missionary in my own Backyard

Living in that area of town and in those apartments did much to prepare me for mission. As a child, I had lived in projects, but I had never lived in this sort of environment before. I still recall the various types of police forces (SWAT, LAPD, local police and others) that came in at six in the morning on a particular Thursday raid to the apartment just outside my window. I saw them push the children up against the wall and hold their hands in the air as they searched the entire group. I saw them take the mother off to jail, and the children were taken into custody of the court. That was one of many times.

I'll never know the impact I had on those children. When I first moved there, I was moving my boxes out of my car and heard that voice from heaven. It said, "Have Bible study with these children."

I laughed. "Lord, I don't do kids," I said. "I don't know anything about kids." I wasn't thinking anything about Bible study. I was moving and getting settled into my new environment and going to seminary to study a very difficult course of work. He told me again, and I agreed to put a plan together for next week when He said, "NOW!" He seems to like that word *Now*!

There were several children outside playing, and I introduced myself and began a nice chat with them. I asked them if they would like to have a Bible study at my apartment. To my BIG surprise, they said, "YES"! I invited them over, and we began the first of seven years of continuous Bible study. One night, I had twenty boys in my living room throwing pillows, fighting, and screaming. I had no idea how to calm them, but somehow I made it through. At Christmas, I had enough gifts for them to pile to the ceiling. Resurrection Day (Easter) celebrations were awesome as well. We had pizza parties, and many times, I would cook or take them to the lake for a BBQ. Sometimes, I would take them to fine restaurants and teach them how to use manners with tablecloths and napkins.

I learned from them as well. I would go inside their homes and pray for them and their families. I learned about lifestyles I had not previously been exposed to before. I learned that many children went all day without eating a meal and went to school being expected to do well in school on empty stomachs. Many homes had no father, and some children had to lift their drunken mother from the floor. I learned that some had fathers who were so addicted to cocaine and alcohol that they just lay down in the stairwell while others walked over them, and their children were embarrassed. I would see the mothers working two or three jobs, trying to make enough to care for her children. Meanwhile, the children left at home would see all sorts of things due to lack of supervision. I saw a mother rush home to get dressed for a party, so she could stay out all night only to go to work the next day. I saw another mother who was clinging on the third father of her four children. I learned about a father who did live with his children but was enraged with anger so much that his children were afraid of him. Their "uncle" as they were told to call him was really their mother's boyfriend, and they actually all lived in the apartment together. I also learned that these kids, despite their troubled home, had a desire to learn about Jesus. They had a desire to do well and be somebody. Many made good grades and had great ambitions. Some thought they would never amount to anything. God placed me in the middle of their lives to make a difference. I was a missionary in my own backyard.

Nilotic Tribe

During school, the president of the student body approached me one day and asked if I would escort a bishop from Kenya to various churches here in America. I gladly said yes, having no idea where Kenya was other than it was an African country. I took the bishop to various churches. We exchanged email information. He invited me to his country.

School was intense. It took two and a half years of rigorous study for two master's degrees. Then, it was time to graduate, and my friend took me to dinner. "What is your plan?" she asked. I couldn't answer her. God had not called me to be pastor over a particular church. He had not called me to a particular nation. He merely had called me as a missionary to the uttermost. My questions were far greater than my answers.

That night, the Lord spoke and said for me to lay down, and He would give me the vision. I grabbed a pencil and paper to write, but I heard nothing for quite some time. I finally gave up thinking it was something I made up instead of something God was going to show me. However, when I closed my eyes that night in June of 2006, a vision of my future played before me like a video.

Birth of Shofar Sound Ministries, Int'l

"I will show you your passion," the Lord said. I saw one hundred acres of land divided into three concepts. There were four gates. The north gate was the main entrance. The headquarters, which also housed the school for missionaries, was located at the south gate. Cottages and land used as a retreat prayer center was at the west gate. At the east gate, the Lord spoke, "Children, discipleship, and poor." Centered between all four gates was a menorah (lampstand) standing at least fifteen feet tall with fire burning from each of its seven candles.

After graduation, I was prompted by the Holy Spirit to contact a bishop in Kenya. He invited me to his country for a mission trip. I raised funds through a few friends, and with very little knowledge of Goma, off I went to work with the bishop and the Nilotic tribe in Northwest Kenya.

The Nilotic tribe is the poorest and most neglected tribe of the forty-two tribes of Kenya. It is estimated that there are over one million Nilotic living in almost 29,729 square miles (77,000 square km) of arid desert. Temperatures are extreme in the 120s, and shade cannot be found. Drought and famine are common amongst the people.

The Nilotics are a nomadic and pastoralist society, primarily herding camels, goats, and sheep. They are well known as fierce warriors. Tribal wars are constantly fought over the stealing of animals, especially at the Ethiopian borders and on the road from Goma to Nairobi, passing through the Baringo tribal territory.

Water is scarce. People walk miles and miles to get a few liters of water, carrying twenty liters on their head, carrying bottles in each hand and pushing twenty liters with their foot. The women and their young children walk 20-30 miles from home in search of water, often returning back to their mud huts with no water. Did I forget to mention they also may not have had any food for the day or perhaps only a small bowl of rice or just the juice of a palm fruit? Often times, as Bishop and I would drive past them on the sandy roads, he would ask me to pick them up and take them to their huts or to give them a bottle of water.

The local fashion in the town of Goma has become more westernized as clothing donations from various countries have made their way in huge quantities to the area. The donations are not distributed freely as we might expect and intended. They are placed in large warehouses and sold to merchandisers who in turn sell the goods at the market for a profit. A pair of used shoes made in the USA can cost more than if you buy them new in America.

Traditional clothing for the Nilotic is animal skin, which is still worn today by some, but most of them wear a shuka, a type of sheet wrapped around the body. It is cool and light. Men wear them, and women in the villages may be seen topless with a wrap around their lower body. In even more rural parts, clothes may not even be worn. It is not unusual to see one bathing naked in a rural area in a small riverbed. In the local town of Goma, there was a man with definite mental issues who walked around naked. His behavior didn't seem to bother anyone. Some laughed at him, and others ignored him.

Disease has overwhelmed the area. Malaria is as common in the Nilotic Tribe as the common cold is in America. Daily, someone dies from malaria. AIDS is prevalent, but one doesn't hear the cause of death in those situation. One merely hears that someone died because he or she was sick. Poor sanitation is also a health threat. There is a lack of toilets, even in the villages nearer to the town. Due to the lack of water, lack of hand washing, and general unclean conditions, there are health concerns. Drought and hunger are too common among the tribal people.

Lack of refrigeration causes roach and rat infestation. One day, I saw the children's meals being kept for them until they came from school. It was tucked away, but had no airtight lid in the 120 degree heat. It was covered with roaches. My food would often be covered with so many flies, it looked like a black cloud hovered over it. It was not unusual for me to eat a fly or two.

At the one hospital that was primitive at best, I visited a baby who had been misdiagnosed. He had been diagnosed with malaria, but he actually had spinal bacterial meningitis. It was too late to treat him properly. He had an IV in his head for antibiotics. His breathing was extremely labored, and he was not wearing any oxygen nor was he on a ventilator. When I arrived, I offered to pay for oxygen, but they said they had none. I offered to pay for to be him heliported to another hospital, but they said there was no way out. I prayed for the baby, and he died one hour later.

I'd heard of the child's illness from the local hardware shop. I had designed a kitchen for Bishop's wife and went to check on the progress. I only had one day left, and I needed the shop to finish the job. It had already taken longer than they told me. I went to assert my position about the delay. That's when I learned the child belonged to the one who was constructing Bishop's wife's kitchen. He was dealing with the child's illness while trying to meet my demands. I realized the man had not gone to the hospital that particular day, so he could finish my order. His child died while he was working on the kitchen. I had no idea it was his child. I went back to the shop and apologized to him and let him know I had prayed for his child. He was extremely delighted that I had gone.

The ICU was a tent with a few mats on the ground and the goats were inside eating. Patients were outside on the cement walkway on mats because there was no room to place them inside. Flies were buzzing around the patients and even going inside of the childrens' noses. It didn't even seem to bother them. They must have been accustomed to the intrusion.

> *"Take the child to her mother," I said. All the children looked at me in silence.*

I stayed in the village at Bishop's hut. The children, sometimes ten to twenty of them, would gather around me at night and sing.

I would tell stories from the Bible and someone who knew a little English would try to translate. I thought it was great that the kids would stay out late with me, but I began to wonder why their parents didn't care that they were out at one in the morning. One night a little one, about three or four years old, was sick with fever. Her sister, who was about eight or nine years old, was caring for her.

"Take the child to her mother," I said. All the children looked at me in silence.

One finally replied, "She has no mother."

Orphans sleep out on the sand near someone's house they knew, slept near the door of the hotel, or any place they could find to try and stay safe at night. In the daytime, they went to hotels searching for food, and they would wander in the

> *One finally replied, "She has no mother."*

streets. Some gathered under a tree, were given a bowl of porridge, and were taught a few lessons from a volunteer teacher. Often the pressure of life was too great, and they succumbed to snorting glue or drinking alcohol. One could see children, even at the age of eight or nine, whose minds were almost totally gone because of the glue and because there was no one to say, "I love you," tuck them in to bed at night, kiss them, hug them, or give them a meal.

One night, a mother did care that her daughter was out. The daughter was just next door when her mother called for her. When she returned home, I could hear the beating. I could hear the screaming, and then, I heard the crack! Her wrist had been broken. The mother told the teenage son to beat her for staying outside. I went to discuss the issue of the beating with the mom. However, it was seen as a proper means of discipline. So, I made no headway. Children are beaten even in school. I am told the government is trying to make some efforts toward new ways of discipline.

Children in the Nilotic Tribe have few if any toys. One kid made himself a toy. He cut a milk carton and attached the lids of a bottle to make the wheels. He pulled it with a string. Clever. He was so happy. He had a toy!

Then, there was the straw that broke the camel's back. I stayed strong seeing poverty at its worst and the environment as I described. However, one day as I was coming out of church, a young boy, about seven years old, was playing in the churchyard. He was running barefoot, as many do, because they have no shoes to wear. However, he was hopping as he ran. I asked Bishop what was wrong with him. He told me in the Nilotic Tribe there were acacia trees, which had large thorns. The thorns were so strong they flatten tires. My vehicle had many flat tires because of those thorns. The boy had one in his foot. I suggested going to the doctor to have it removed, but Bishop said there was no one to pay the bill. No matter what I suggested, it seemed useless. Then, my tears came, and I couldn't stop them. I felt the sense of hopelessness and helplessness for the children. Yet, they continued to play and hop, smile as they walked, search for water, and sing for Jesus at night under the stars even though they were sick and homeless orphans. Bishop just pushed me into the car and said, "Chara, we trust Jesus."

I asked myself, "What can one woman do?"

I asked myself, "What can one woman do?" After six weeks on the ground in that rural area, where life-threatening poverty was staring me in the face, Shofar Sound Ministries, Int'l was born.

6

God's Calling is Personal

In John 11:20-29, Martha met Jesus as he arrived at the home of Martha, Mary, and Lazarus. Lazarus had died. Jesus had a conversation with Martha and then asks specifically for Mary. *"The master is come and calleth for thee."* God's call was a personal call.

Isaiah 43:1 says, *"... I have called thee by thy name; thou art mine."* When God called Samuel in 1 Samuel 3, He called him by his name.

There are two problems in the church related to the area of *calling*. First, there are those who refuse to answer the call. Then, there are those who think they are called to some service because someone told them they are called. Everyone is called to do something, but some want to do service that God didn't call them to do.

It is a very serious matter to be called by God into service or for an assignment. To refuse the call is not only to refuse to obey God, but to refuse to serve Him in the purpose He designated for you. Your life will be void, empty, and unfulfilled. You will always have a longing inside that can never be complete. You will search far and wide and never be able to feel satisfied. You will try other jobs; you may even turn to alcohol, drugs, or various lifestyles in search for fulfillment of purpose.

Jonah refused to obey God's call to go and preach against Nineveh. He found himself in the midst of a huge storm and then in the belly of a big fish. God's grace and mercy rescued him, so the mission could be completed. That's our God!

Those who think they are called because their momma or daddy or their preacher prophesied to them what they were going to be are not much different from those who refused to obey. Maybe, they decided to do it because of what momma said. The problem here is that they are still not walking in the will of God.

If someone is doing something he or she is not called to do, then what is it that he or she is neglecting? The result is the same as refusing their true calling. They may be obeying momma, but they are not obeying God. It is different if they become a pastor because momma saw them as a pastor when they were chldren, and God later called them to be a pastor. They can't really walk in the calling of a pastor until they have heard it from God Himself. If they are using their own skills, talents, and abilities to be the pastor without the call of God on their life, the empire will fall. It cannot prosper. They may have a business sense to set up an organization. They may have skills to motivate people and rally people to give financially, but if they are not called by God to pastor, the empire will fall. Those skills and talents were God given for perhaps another purpose in the Kingdom.

Oftentimes, people view the role of pastor as a high-level position, a lofty perch, or position of great influence. Although it *is* a position of great influence, some people want the position merely to be in charge, have authority, and get recognition. Many see the position as a place of power and prestige. Oftentimes, we see people who want this position and are not called to it abuse the position. The pastor is actually the role of a servant—one called to serve God's people. Those who are truly called usually struggle to say "Yes" because they recognize the sacrifice, dedication, and commitment required.

I was in a meeting one day when pastors were individually asked to tell the group about their calling. I was so shocked that only a few could say God had called them. Most gave a story of their preacher or mother telling them, when they were children, they would become a preacher. This may be a part of confirmation, but it is *not* the calling. Was there a dream, a Scripture that dramatically stood out, or a message that the Holy Spirit ministered to their Spirit one day? Most often, one will know the *time* and the *place*, the *story* and the *circumstance*. God's call is personal, and He makes it known, and He is clear about it. He doesn't have to yell it to them. He may just whisper it, but they will *know*.

In Acts 9, Saul (later known as Apostle Paul) was on his way to Damascus to kill the Christians. Suddenly, a voice came to him, *"Saul, Saul, why persecutest thou me?"* God called Saul by name and had a tremendous purpose for his life. God called Moses in Exodus 3:4, *"…Moses, Moses. And he said, Here am I."*

When God called me, He called me by my name. He said, "Chara, go. For this may be your last chance." I knew He was talking to *me*. He called my name. I knew He wasn't talking to the person next to me on the pew. I knew when I came back from the altar no one else could hear or understand what I was experiencing and hearing at that moment. It was for *me*. It wasn't for them to hear. It was between Him and *me* that day.

When God calls you into service, you will know God means *you* and is not talking to anyone else. You will not think he means your sister or brother or cousin. God will make it clear, and the call will be personal. Some describe the calling as hearing the voice; others describe it as a feeling, a sense, a sensation, an absolute knowing, a whisper, or an impression. It may be hard to put into words because it is from the Holy Spirit. The Holy Spirit ministers in "unearthly" ways that many non-believers would call "crazy." Yet, when the Spirit speaks to you, you know beyond your imagination and beyond any shadow of a doubt. There is an agreement in your Spirit. There is peace and joy.

Samuel was not clear at first that it was God calling him (1 Samuel 3). He thought it was the priest Eli calling him. He had not yet learned to hear the voice of God clearly. Samuel was young, but God kept calling. Although he thought he was answering Eli, Samuel gave the right response. He said, "Here am I."

God not only kept calling, but he placed the right person in Samuel's path to help him understand the call. Eli realized it was God calling and told Samuel in Verse 9 to answer God by saying, *"Speak, Lord; for thy servant heareth."* Samuel's mother, Hannah, probably had told Samuel that he would be a servant of God. She had wanted a son and prayed so hard for him. She vowed if God gave her a son she would give him back to God. Even though Hannah knew what she had vowed and perhaps had told Samuel, he still had to receive his calling from God.

God Calls in Many Ways

God is not limited to how, why, who, and when He calls. God is all-knowing and His ways are greater than our ways (Isaiah 55:8). He sees beyond what we see. He is God, and He is creator. He has destined you for purpose.

He speaks through dreams as He did with Joseph in Genesis 37. God calls through providence or God-guided circumstances. In 2 Kings 5, a little maid had been taken into captivity out of Israel and placed as a servant to wait on Naaman's wife. Naaman was a mighty man of valor, a captain in the Syrian army. The young handmaiden was called by providence. It was not an accident that she was the one chosen to be the slave girl, taken into captivity from the Syrian Army. It was not just happenstance. No, it was the providence of God that she had been called. He had placed her there with an assignment and purpose. She may not have even realized that she was there for a reason. She was simply serving with humility. Yet, it was through her humility and boldness that Naaman could be cured of leprosy and be delivered from pride and idolatry.

God is not limited to how, why, who, and when He calls.

He calls in a time of sickness and even during death as with Mary in John 11. He calls in unusual circumstances like with Moses through a burning bush in Exodus 3.

God calls people through His Word. He speaks through preaching, through people, through angels, and any way He

70

chooses. Almost always, if not always, God's call will be confirmed in His Word. He will back up His calling through the Scripture.

John 16:13 tells us the Holy Spirit will guide us into all truth and show us things to come. Psalms 32:8 says, *"He will instruct you and teach you in the way you should go."*

God Equips Those He Calls

Hebrews 13:20-21 (KJV) says,
"Now the God of peace, that brought again from the dead our Lord Jesus, that great shepherd of the sheep, through the blood of the everlasting covenant,
Make you perfect in every good work to do his will, working in you that which is well pleasing in his sight, through Jesus Christ; to whom be glory for ever and ever. Amen."

I'd like to draw your attention to the word "perfect." In the Biblical Greek, this word is *katartisai* (transliterated). It means to equip. It carries the idea of complete equipment or preparation. God has completely equipped and prepared you to do the purpose He has called you to do. The ability to do the job has already been established inside of your spiritual DNA. God has already given you everything you need to walk out your calling.

The equipping still has to manifest in the natural. This is why most people say they want to be called but are hesitant because they know they would have to go through something transformational to become equipped or to receive the equipment to carry out that call. Therefore, many just bow their heads and walk away. In the Bible, we have many examples of those who did not walk away. They allowed God to bring out the equipment to manifest the full potential in their life.

Let's take Joseph, for instance. God called Joseph in a dream when he was a young teenager. The dream was not fulfilled until later in his adult life. He had many lessons to learn, though the equipment was inside of him in his spiritual DNA. God had given it to him, but then, it had to be realized. God had to equip him in the natural for the full assignment.

All along the way, Joseph did great things. He served Potiphar's house, and he interpreted dreams in prison, but God had more for him. I am sure many times Joseph must have said, "I don't know why I'm going through this situation at this moment, but I do know I'm going through it for a reason."

Joseph merely had a dream. Yet, it was the dream that kept him living; that dream that kept him persevering and enduring toward the greater purpose and the greater work he knew he had been called to do. He didn't know what it looked like nor did he know when he would get there or where that would be. He didn't know anything except God gave him a dream. That dream was so powerful because it gave him the "*know.*" He knew it was from God. He knew God was faithful to His promises and He wouldn't fail him. He knew God had done it for others. He knew that so deep in his spirit that nothing could move him or shake him. No matter what circumstance came his way, he knew God would bring him through because there was a call on his life.

Knowing is the First Step of Preparation

Knowing is the seed God planted inside of you when He called you. It is the assurance you have that God is the one who called you, and that assurance will carry you through all the trials, tests, and sufferings you must endure to make it to the finish line.

All the experiences of Joseph's entire life were building blocks for his final destination or his ultimate call to the palace. His purpose was to save his family during a horrible famine. Those were the same family of brothers that had tried to kill him, sold him into slavery, placed him into a pit, and left him for dead. Joseph also was wrongly accused by Potiphar's wife, was removed from a high level position, and put in prison. It was in prison that Joseph realized he could interpret dreams. In prison, he would meet and interpret the dreams of the cupbearer and the baker. Through that interaction, doors were open for Joseph. The pits and the prisons in your life help to strengthen our character and prepare you for your palace assignment. Joseph was willing to let God use him during the worst of circumstances. He was probably not fully aware that he was being set up by God to take him to his higher calling, but he had faith and answered his call.

Knowing What Moves You and Motivates You Helps to Guide You to Your Purpose

Recognizing your interests and inspirations help you to

identify your gifts. I never anticipated God would give me some very unique gifts. I could not have imagined casting out demons from people. I'd always been interested in how fortune tellers thought they could tell the future and things of that nature, but I never realized God would turn my secular interest into the truth about the spirit realm.

My dad, of course, preached about hell and the devil, but the spirit world was not overly emphasized. He would preach about Jesus and the disciples casting out demons and spoke that it was definitely biblical. He wasn't a pastor who frequently laid hands on people; he didn't speak in tongues, nor did he speak often about casting out demons. Yet, I was still very interested.

I can now see how God touched my heart as a young girl and how he gradually moved me into my gifting. Little did I realize I would need the gifting when going into the uttermost parts of the world. I would lay hands on a witch doctor in Thailand, work with many who dealt in the occult in the USA and in the foreign countries, and go into pagan lands where people worshipped trees and animals. In seminary, I took as many spiritual warfare courses as possible to try to understand the biblical approach to demons and evil spirits. However, it never ever dawned on me that I would be gifted in this area to actually cast demons out of people.

Knowing When and How to Move Takes Faith And Courage

Activating your gifts is a *by-faith* endeavor. God prepares the way for you. God's schooling is different than college preparation. Sometimes, the way God teaches you is simply by putting you in a certain situation or by giving you a particular opportunity. Usually, the situation is one you would not have stepped into unless you had to. You step out by faith knowing that the situation is from God and that He will show you what to do and how to do it. He may give you several classes.

> *God's schooling is different than college preparation.*

Joseph stepped out by faith. When he was in prison, the cupbearer and the baker were in prison with him, and they had dreams. First, Joseph recognized the men were troubled, and then, he asked them if God is not the interpreter of dreams. Then, Joseph courageously interpreted the dreams. It took faith and courage to act on what God placed inside him. What if he was wrong? What if God struck him dead for doing what God and only God was known to do? The list of "what if's?" can go on and on. Joseph was willing and obedient to speak. If we are willing and obedient, then we can have the fruit of the land (Isaiah 1:19).

We can probably say Joseph was not experienced in interpreting dreams, yet God provided an opportunity for him to learn because his eventual dream interpretation experience would lead to fulfillment of his destiny and to his calling. Joseph listened to God and moved in obedience; then, God trained him. If Joseph had been too afraid to move when given the opportunity, he might never have reached fulfillment of his dreams.

I learned the first time I cast out a demon that God taught me one thing, and the next time, I learned something else. It was a continual process. However, the greatest gift of all is the ability to hear and then to act when God speaks. Obedience is key to operating in your gift.

In 2005, just before I went on a mission trip to the Philippines, I was an associate pastor of a Filipino church. We were asked to come and pray for Imelda, a lady who had been sick for several weeks and had missed work. Nothing was helping her to get better.

When we arrived inside her home, she was sitting in a recliner. Her coloring was very grey, which was strange for a Filipina. The senior pastor, Pastor Mabuhay, asked me to lay hands on her and pray for her. The others would gather around me and pray as well. That was one of my first times to lay hands on someone, so I just held out my hands.

"Sister," I said, "we come to you in the love of Jesus, and by His stripes you are healed." I laid my right hand on her forehead. I felt a streak of intense heat leave my hand. I couldn't explain it, but I knew it was from the Holy Spirit. As soon as I touched her forehead, her body began to shake violently. So much so that she shook out of the recliner. Not knowing what else to do, I just kept my hand on her. I could tell by then that was not just an illness but a spiritual situation. As she lay on the floor, I said in a commanding voice, "Demon, come out of her in the name of Jesus." Instantly, her head bowed backwards, and her body arched. The demon spoke in a different voice to me. I don't remember exactly what vulgarities it yelled, but it was not nice! I continued to keep my hands on her, commanding the demon out in the name of Jesus.

I could see the demon moving in her belly. It was as if the lady was pregnant with an oversized child, and it was doing flip-flops inside. After quite some time, one demon after another left the woman's body, and she lay exhausted on the floor. We all continued to pray over her, and then, she woke up wondering what had happened. She returned to her recliner, her color became normal almost instantly, and the next day, she returned to work. I too was exhausted because it was literally work!

More than the work was the power that had come over me. It was not merely a physical power, but a spiritual strength and boldness I had never experienced. Afterwards, I went to the corner to be alone for a few minutes. It seemed as though I needed to release that power back to heaven. I use those words because that is what it felt like. I began to travail loudly and lifted my hands to God. I glorified Him by myself for a few moments and rejoined the group. We all prayed together and rejoiced in the Lord and His marvelous works. I realized God had taken me through first grade or Spiritual Warfare 101 that day. I can say that now because that experience was mild compared to others He has used to teach me. I consider each time a training experience because none of them were ever the same. There were many things that were similar, but the experience was never the same.

I would come to learn that I needed this gift while on "mission in the uttermost". While on the mission field in the Philippines, I was asked to pray for a young man named Jose. Ailene, my host, and I were walking past him, and she said, "You need to pray for him." I said I would do that right away. I didn't know anything about Jose. As I approached him and he agreed, I looked into his eyes. It was as if I were drawn to his eyes. I could see into the back of his eyes. I had not ever experienced that before, but I knew I could see a demon. It sounded crazy to me too.

As I approached Ailene, I told her I needed to work with him and pray for him again; I told her I saw a demon in his eyes. She said, "How do you know?" I replied, "I don't know, but I know I saw him."

The next evening was my last night. I was disappointed because it was my last night, and I did not see the young man in the audience. However, after church services were over and I was walking out of the building, I felt a strange supernatural pull to my right. I turned. The sensation was like his spirit was trying to get my attention. There was Jose sitting far off on the right side of the church. He was staring at me. I walked and greeted him.

"Do you love Jesus?" I asked him. That's how it started.

"Ma'am, I don't know," he said. "My mind is scrambled." I asked him to just say he loves Jesus with his mouth even if he didn't know. The young man tried, but when he spoke the words, his body began to jerk uncontrollably. He jerked so hard he fell to the floor. I called for the other pastors to help me. We began praying for him. His entire body torqued. He hit and bit, but we kept calling on the name of Jesus, commanding the evil spirits to leave him. All sorts of demonic sounds and growls came from him. There were seven of us working on him. His body was so strong it took all of us to hold him down and keep him from hurting himself. His voice changed, and the demons said evil things to us. We worked with him for about four hours before he took some bands off of his right wrist and threw them across the room. I learned he had been dealing in sorcery, and those amulets came from his witch doctor.

He was cleansed. He lay on the floor as though he had been through the most exhausting experience of his life. He had experienced a spiritual surgery. Afterward, he looked at total peace and was calm. He was dazed, but he got up as if nothing had happened. I walked with him and asked how he felt. He said, "No more scramble, ma'am. No more scramble." I was informed months later that he was diligently serving the Lord.

You may think that type of ordeal happens only in the village areas of foreign lands. Oh no!

I was called to the home of a young woman named Cynthia. She was a heroin addict and also abused alcohol. She would sleep on the floor of the bathroom while curled up in a fetal position. Her brother, John, went with me to her home. We picked her up from the bathroom floor and sat her on the bed. We asked her if she would just acknowledge Jesus as Lord and Savior of her life. She could barely talk, but God knew and saw her heart. She wanted to be set free.

Her room was dark. It was decorated with black curtains, black bed linens, a Ouija board, and all sorts of heavy metal music, and demonic items were visible in her room. I asked her to demonstrate her desire to be free by getting rid of those items. It took her a while, but she began to throw away these items and destroy them. Her brother and I just prayed as we watched her begin the process. When she had finished cleaning the room, I laid hands on her and began to pray. Her body began to shake.

"There he is; he is in my closet!" she exclaimed. She was

seeing the demons in her room and could hear their voices. We commanded them to stop their behavior, and they did—in the name of Jesus! As John and I began praying for her, her strength increased. Controlling her was difficult because there were only two of us holding her and keeping her from hitting her head on the floor. Her entire body would flip up in the air and land in a totally different position. She would let out shrill screams of demonic sounds as the demons left her. Her head turned all the way to the back, and she gasped for air. We commanded that the spirit of death leave her in the name of Jesus — instantly her head flew back to the front as she gulped a huge gulp of air.

We worked with her for six hours non-stop. When she experienced her deliverance, she "awoke," for lack of another word to describe it. She acted as though she had no idea of what had happened. She went outside to the backyard and couldn't believe she was able to go into the light. She had not been able to stand daylight in such a long time. She sat outside for a bit just enjoying nature. She described colors, saying before that day she had not been able to see color; she said the world was only visible to her in shades of black and grey. Then, she did something very strange.

Cynthia took me to the bathroom and opened the drawers. She ran her fingers up and down the seams of the cabinet. She pulled out needles and syringes. She took me out to the car and did the same to the seams in the roofing and then to the refrigerator in the garage and pulled needles and syringes out of the coils in the back of it. I didn't know there were so many hiding places for the insulin-like syringes.

After we completed the housecleaning, we opened the front door. It seemed as though the demons left the house and ran up the street. Not even a minute after we opened the door, there was a car crash just a few yards up the street. Only two cars were on the street. One car was being driven erratically, and the other car came from the left side street. They collided with each other. Here was yet another lesson God taught me. I learned when casting out demons, I must send the demons somewhere, so they cannot hurt anyone else and cannot be allowed to roam anymore.

Monkey Spirits

Another example of how God taught me when and how to move was when I was on the mission field. Because I had been invited to preach at a large church in Africa, I left Goma early. While in Africa, I was introduced to Kanisa, a lady who owned a travel agency. She invited me to lunch. She talked to me about her nephew and his condition and asked if I would go to her home and evaluate him.

When I went to observe Abdul, a twelve-year-old boy, I was simply dumbfounded. He was not able to talk; he just made sounds like a monkey. He jumped just like a monkey from chair to couch and back and forth. When given crackers to eat, he ate the entire box within minutes. He put them on the table and ate them from the table pushing and shoving them into his mouth. When I tried to take the box of crackers away, he got very angry.

I observed his behavior for about an hour and then decided to test the spirits in order to determine if it was an illness of sorts or a spirit. I pulled out a cross I had brought with me. I held it in front of Abdul, and he screamed with a shrill voice. I tried again, and then, he took the cross from my hand and snapped it in half.

Often I use salt as a weapon against the enemy. The Bible says we are the salt of the earth (Matthew 5:13). Salt heals, purifies, and cleanses; therefore, it is a symbol the enemy does not like in the spiritual realm. Salt and olive oil are two powerful agents used in casting out demons. They have no magical properties. They are merely salt and olive oil, but we use them as symbols. In the spiritual arena, these elements represent the Holy Spirit. The demonic spirits find them offensive and react violently to them.

When I brought out the box of salt, the evil spirits in the child began to react to it. I poured some out on the table where he had eaten the crackers. He reacted with anger, and forcefully and agressivly wiped the salt off the table onto the floor.

As I continued to assess the child, I asked when this behavior began and what were the circumstances relating to it. I was informed the mother had converted from Catholicism to Islam when she married a man of the Islamic faith. She later decided to leave the father for reasons unknown to me. Her mother-in-law told her if she left her husband, the child would be under a curse and he would never be a child. African pastors had informed me that when the Imam of the mosque prays, he sends evil spirits to those who have converted or betrayed their faith. The pastors informed me they had seen essentially three major outcomes. The person becomes like a monkey, a crocodile, or a snake. In that case, Abdul developed the behavior of a monkey.

I realized his deliverance called for something greater than I could do alone. I asked the family to bring the child to the church on Sunday. I arranged for the pastors to help me. There were six of us: five strong African men and me. As we began to pray for Abdul, the spirits became very angry. They growled and fought with supernatural strength. It took all of us to hold the twelve year old down—and we could not succeed! He got loose each time. We had to hold him down to prevent him from hurting himself during the ordeal. We worked for several hours on the child, but too many rebellious spirits were working against us. We agreed we would have to pray and fast for days, but the aunt never brought the child back.

Some people would consider that a failed attempt. God has perfect timing and perfect precision. My job is just to be available and obedient and learn what God is teaching me. I now know the value of fasting and praying as a spiritual discipline.

I could write an entire book on the many deliverances I have participated in, but I think you get the point. God gifts you according to your calling. God called me to the uttermost, and I needed this gift if I were to go into the uttermost where I would encounter darkness, witchcraft, magic, and other forms of the occult.

What is the Uttermost?

By now you must be asking, "What is the uttermost?"

In the Greek, the word is "*eschatos.*" It means the last, the end, the ends of the earth, or the extreme. I was called to those whose life situations are extreme, to those who may feel they are at the end and have no hope. That can be in the USA, in Africa,

Europe, in Asia, or anywhere. Everyone has a different calling. One calling is not more or less important than another. Some are more dangerous and require more gifts and sacrifice, but none is insignificant in God's eyes.

Not everyone is called to the uttermost. The Filipino lady Ailene, I discussed earlier, who had not been to work for a month, had a husband who was a pastor. He said he had laid hands on his wife, had commanded the demons out in Jesus' name, but she still had not improved. I too have prayed for people in certain situations and seemingly nothing happened.

It takes a certain anointing for each calling. Called to the uttermost requires an anointing that many others don't understand. For this reason, you must not listen to people. People don't know or understand your calling or your gifting. You must be tuned into the voice of the Lord and follow only His voice. For example, I was impressed by the Lord to go to Egypt. No one could understand why I would want to go to Egypt so soon after the riots where unrest still existed. I couldn't listen to them. I knew I had the call to go. I was even told that I was just a one-woman show and should let the big mission agencies go.

Were they saying God couldn't use one person? Were they saying I was insignificant? What were they saying? It didn't matter. Nothing could stop me. God told me to go, so I did.

You must go where God is calling you and do what He tells you. You cannot walk in your calling if you are going to listen to people instead of God. God does speak through people, but not in this manner. I too have questioned the Lord as to why He sends me into the uttermost when in fact many Christians are there. I have questioned why they can't do whatever needs to be done. However, only God knows why He will send a certain one far away to a special task or mission. Who are we to question? God's ways are higher than ours, and His thoughts are greater than ours. You must just be willing to go where He calls you to go and do what He tells you to do. All too frequently, I have been told things like, "We have been waiting for you" or "We have tried that so many times before without results." No, I am not better than anyone or special. It is just that I walk in my calling. I know when God calls me to a particular mission, He is about to do something. It has nothing to do with me, except that I am willing to go, willing to sacrifice, willing to be used, willing to be the only one, willing to be isolated from the world of naysayers, and willing to trust Him.

Your calling requires sacrifice, commitment, and determination that no one else can understand because it is your calling, not theirs.

"I'm glad God called you and not me." I get this comment about my ministry quite often. Being called to the mission field is an extremely distinctive and challenging calling. The person of a missionary has a unique personality and many attributes. These qualities enable the person to perform under circumstances that are beyond many people's comprehension.

Have you heard your calling yet? Did you answer it?

7

What is the Call to be a Missionary?

The role of the missionary is to live and work among cultures different than your own in order to administer the *missio dei* (the mission of God).

The word *missionary* does not appear in the Bible. In its truest sense, it is the word *apostle* in the Bible. A missionary, *apostolos,* in the Greek, is a messenger, a delegate; one who is sent forth with orders (Strong's Concordance #652). I think Apostle Paul was the greatest missionary in the Bible. His missionary journeys depict the very challenges and dangers that may arise on the mission field.

To be in the best position to communicate the Gospel, a true missionary must live and work among the people in order to build relationships and understand the culture. How can you communicate the Gospel effectively if you don't explain it from a cultural context? For instance, the Bible talks about many types of animals. What if you are in a far-away village reading the Bible from a Western context? Suppose the local people have no understanding of a certain animal that is mentioned in a Bible story. A missionary who lives and works among the villagers would use a similar animal from the villagers' context, so they can have a better understanding. And what would angels look like in a Thai context or African context? How would they visualize Jesus? Would He look like the Jesus we see in our interpretative art? Of course not!

A missionary may operate in all five-fold ministries (Ephesians 4:11) in order to face the dangers of the field. The missionary may speak in tongues, may have the power to cast out demons, and *must* have the extraordinary gift of faith. They may possess astonishing boldness and courage, have the gift of discernment, have supernatural dreams and visions, and may be able to interpret dreams and visions. Some also may prophecy, speak, and may warn and encourage. The list can go on and on because God fully equips those whom He has called. The greater the risks of the assignment, the more gifts are necessary and are given.

Being called to the uttermost requires one to live a holy life without wavering. It requires operation of all the gifts at some time or another, and it requires absolute surrender and dependence on God. Many times missionaries called to the uttermost have had to give up all they owned; they may have left their jobs to follow the calling. Oftentimes, especially if gifted in the prophetic, the missionary stands alone, lives in solitude, and is too often misunderstood. Sometimes, the loneliness and isolation presents challenges to the missionary, yet it is part of the preparation for the journey.

> *The greater the risks of the assignment, the more gifts are necessary and are given.*

Evangelists are sometimes mistaken for missionaries. The evangelist, *euaggelistes* in the Greek (Strong's #2099), is a bringer of good tidings. They are New Testament proclaimers of salvation through Jesus, but they are not apostles. An evangelist proclaims an evangelistic message often travelling from place to place asserting the Gospel of salvation. They move in and out and are usually based in their own culture. Those that do travel abroad do not participate in the culture to a large extent. They may go to the country, stay in a hotel or with a pastor, preach and leave. Sightseeing is not considered living and working among the culture although it may give the evangelist a bit of insight into the lives of others rather than their own. Let's take a deeper look into the distinctive characteristics of mission, and you will readily see the difference.

Mission Is:
A Passion to Carry the Gospel No Matter How You Have to get There

Elephant Ride

Transportation challenges do not stop the missionary. The missionary is creative and will find and use any means to get to the destination. As a missionary called to the uttermost, I often do not know how I will get to many of the places I go. I was in Thailand near the border of Burma. I needed to go inside the jungle to an animistic tribe. One missionary in Thailand had been ministering there for years, but that would be the first time in all those years that anyone in the tribe had come to accept Jesus.

The missionary was going to baptize a few of them, and I joined his team to offer my gifts in ministry, especially those of spiritual warfare and healing.

The problem for me was one of distance: the village was six hours by foot up and down steep mountains in very hot and humid temperatures. My feet and stamina would not allow that sort of travel. What would I do? It was during the rainy season, so motorcycles were out of the question. Slippery steep slopes and clay-like paths would be too dangerous. Cars were not an option in the jungle. But elephants --- wild jungle elephants, not tourist elephants, were the only feasible option. So, I hired an elephant to take me six hours up and down the mountains. The driver would sit on the elephant's ears, and I would sit in a bamboo basket placed on a huge chain used to keep the elephant from running. Well, a missionary makes the best of a bad situation.

But first, I had to board the elephant. I climbed on a table, so I could push myself up, but that angered the elephant, so I quit that very quickly. The driver lowered the elephant and told me to climb onto the elephant's ears. I couldn't; I just couldn't. I felt like I would hurt the elephant. Well, how would you like someone climbing on *your* ears?

Finally, a group of guys lifted me up, and I climbed into my basket. It was a scary ordeal. I felt really high up on the huge elephant. The others in the team walked on ahead, and I was left alone with the elephant and the driver. The elephant driver and I could not communicate because he spoke no English, and I spoke no Thai. For six hours, I couldn't get off of the elephant. I was thirsty because the jungle was so hot, but I couldn't get down to use the toilet (or use a bush). As we passed through the dense jungle, I made the most of it. Because I was level with the treetops, I picked bananas from the trees. As the elephant slowly clumped along, he would just uproot a tree and devour the entire tree in minutes. Ants and spiders and other creatures fell on my body as we pushed through the forest. The backs of my legs were torn from rubbing on the bamboo basket. That was just a few hours in the life of one called to the uttermost.

On the way through the jungle on the elephant, the driver stopped to talk to a couple of men. They began speaking in their local language, which I didn't understand and felt no need to pay attention. Then, I heard one of the men's voices getting louder and louder as if he were addressing me. I looked at him and realized he *was* talking to me. At first, I couldn't understand the English through the heavy accent. He happened to be a jungle military policeman and wanted to know where I was going and why. I could have been arrested for not responding quickly. They also had never seen an American in the jungle on an elephant. I explained my mission, and we continued on our way.

I had forgotten that elephants spews their trunk and squirts water on their body to keep cool. It wasn't long before I remembered. Totally unprepared, I felt the fluid in my face, my eyes, and my body. Yuck! And, I didn't have a towel to wipe my eyes.

For six hours, I held my urges and finally made it there without any embarrassing incidents.

On the trip back, I remembered to take a towel. It came in handy. A rainstorm came, and the towel was all that I had. I made the best of a bad situation. Why not just have fun? I surrender to these challenges.

In the mountains, we passed several little villages and the people, especially the children, would run out to see the white lady riding through their village in the mountain on an elephant. I would wave and greet the people. When the rain came, I decided to have fun. I pretended I was the queen being brought into the city on my elephant. I wrapped the towel around my head like a crown, and I greeted everyone waving my hand and speaking to all the villagers. Mommas, babies, children and all ran out to see me, laughing and greeting me. "I am a missionary," I told them, "and I have a message for you. Jesus loves you." The elephant provided me with the opportunity to spread the message of Jesus Christ to a people that needed to be ministered to, delivered, and healed. An elephant helped me get there.

Get in the Boat

That wasn't the only strange type of transportation I've had to use. When in Kenya, the Lord impressed upon me to go to Uganda. Most would take a bus and go to the city or fly and enter through the wide gates. I, however, am called to the uttermost, also known as the narrow gate. Bishop, his wife, and I boarded a bus. Our legs were cramped in a small space for about twenty-four hours with chickens and cargo under our feet. Our top heavy bus, packed down with vegetables, goats, chickens, and luggage, was headed out to Port Victoria, in the mountains. We were there to open a church and ordain two pastors. The Uganda border was across Lake Victoria. Shofar Sound would pay for the boat that would take us on a three-hour journey to cross the lake.

We had a large team going to Uganda. Then, we saw the boat; it was a canoe! A canoe, really? If that wasn't bad enough, I was told the boat had a leak. I asked if there was another boat available. Of course not!

Then, I asked for a confirmation from everyone, "Did God tell us to go to Uganda?" All agreed that was true.

"Then, get in the boat," I said.

"Chara, you have no fear," Bishop said. I told him I had fear, but God told us to go and that was the boat He gave us, so we had to get in the boat. Three hours later, we arrived in the primitive town. That night, that same leaking boat got us back to Kenya without any problem.

Mission Is: Eating Provisions You Don't Know or Like Under Situations or Severe Circumstances

For the westerner, food and sanitation are often major trepidations when travelling overseas. However, food varieties and sanitation matters do not disturb the missionary. One of the true signs of a missionary is the ability to eat or try various ethnic and adventurous foods. A missionary often has to eat foods that no one in the western world could imagine eating.

Even before I fulfilled my calling, God trained me. I was stationed in the Philippines where I was served dog on many occasions. Dog is absolutely not something I would order in a restaurant or cook at home. However, my intrinsic personality liked adventurous and daring situations. I liked to challenge myself by doing the things that only a few would do. Without that characteristic, I probably couldn't survive as a missionary.

The kitchens in the Philippines were often outdoors. I walked around the house where the women were cooking outside to find them skinning dogs and chopping them up. That was only one of the many exciting dishes I have had to eat. In some situations, I ate the dish because it would have been an insult to the people to refuse. They may have spent their last little bit of money to prepare a meal for me, or perhaps, it was all they had to give. I have had to eat alligator, octopus, duck feet, snails, (not escargot with garlic and served elegantly in a restaurant, although I have had that too), turtle, cow testicle soup, jungle rat, camel back, goat and ugali, eggs left in 120 degree heat all day, flies that swarmed my food, and many others.

While you may be experiencing some unpleasant physical symptoms as I discuss this aspect of being a missionary, someone else may be getting excited about the possibility of the experience. One thing for sure is that a missionary has to truly surrender. As a missionary, I have had to absolutely trust God to keep me safe from illness. Sanitary conditions in most villages in the uttermost are not like those in America. I had to drink water that was black and impure. I had a bottle with a purifier and some tablets to put in the water, but just imagine seeing black water and praying that the filter system on the cup was really working.

One funny, but really sad story about my unique food experiences was with Bishop and a group of pastors in South

Sudan. The land was scorched from the sun and cracked from the drought. The huge cracks were so large you could fall inside. On our way to the village, we stopped for dinner at the only place available: an open hut with a thatched roof. Although I had been in Africa several times, it seemed that my mind lapsed during that visit. I asked for a menu! The server told me the menu was goat and ugali. Ugali is a very fine corn meal boiled into a moist bread like substance. You take a small amount, roll it into a ball, and eat it dipped into the soup of the meal, adding a bit of meat or vegetable to it. I asked if there was any cabbage, a favorite in Kenya. I was told the menu was goat and ugali. I asked if there was any other vegetable. I was told, "Ma'am, the menu is goat and ugali."

So, my meal was goat and ugali.

The next day, we were travelling back through the area, and that was still the only restaurant available. I must have lost my mind. I asked what the menu was for that day. I, for some reason in my Western mind, wanted and believed it may have changed. But no, the server told me the menu was goat and ugali. I asked if there was a vegetable that day.

"Ma'am," she answered, "the menu today is goat and ugali. The menu yesterday was goat and ugali; the menu tomorrow will be goat and ugali." Needless to say, I had goat and ugali.

You Got One

"Ha, you got one!" Bishop said to me when I swallowed a fly. My meal had been served and placed on the coffee table in the mud hut. Hunger was not only prevalent in the people, but also in the animals and even the flies. Three cats were on the table, all attempting to get to my food. These cats were small in size but had the personality of lions. I was trying to push the cats away and take a little of my food at the same time without getting bitten. Flies covered my food like a black frosting. I guess you could say I had "blackened ugali." Those flies were persistent and determined. They were the kind that stuck to you and didn't care if they were being shooed off. They were slow and stung when they landed on your skin. I tried to shoo off the many flies that covered my plate. The flies were stubborn as I grabbed a little food with my fingers, as is the customary dining etiquette in many areas of third world countries. I was rushing to get it in my mouth as I fought the cats off. I didn't pay enough attention to what was going inside. All of a sudden, I felt something flying in my mouth. I was trying my best to have table manners and not react because that was my first trip to Goma. I wanted to be a strong missionary and not show any response. My face changed, and I tried to let the fly out of my mouth, but it went down my esophagus with the rest of the ugali. Bishop noticed it and made his comment as if it were a common occurrence.

It really was. It wasn't the last time I had to eat a fly! They cover your cup of tea. Even if you try to cover the tea, you aren't fast enough. Yep, a few went down. It is amazing how God prepares and equips the one He sends or appoints to a calling. He never calls you without equipping you. You may be saying, "No way. I can't do that." Well, do you think I would have had the courage to go if someone would have told me that I would eat flies— and not chocolate covered ones either?

Not every missionary has to experience the extreme, but when you are called to the uttermost, the extreme is where you like to live. I thrive in the extreme.

Mission Is:
Power to Proclaim Liberty and
Healing in the Name of Jesus Christ

The missionary is not devastated by disease, illnesses, and death. While I was travelling in the Philippines, on our way to a village, the Lord impressed upon me to stop and pray for people at the local hospital. The other team members said we didn't have time and could do it on the way back. I couldn't let it rest until I entered the hospital. I didn't know why I was there, but I knew I was led by the Holy Spirit, who whispered my assignment to me, and interestingly enough, only to me. No one else could understand, so I had to assert my request. After receiving permission to do so, my host and I went around the hospital asking to pray with patients. The hospital was full and patients were lined up in beds in the hallways. I approached the bed of one young lady who was seemed to be in distress. I asked about the situation and if I could pray with her. She told me she was pregnant and was losing the baby. She was bleeding profusely, and no one had her blood type. There was no blood bank, and she left bleeding out, left to die. She was given a few hours, if that, to live.

A power came over me so strong causing me to throw my hand back and then forward, pointing my finger directly at her, declaring, "In the name of Jesus Christ of Nazareth, send someone right now with her blood type and save her life." It was in that instant that a Filipino soldier walked into the hospital from a nearby military camp. He said he heard the hospital was looking for someone with his rare blood type and wanted to donate. My assignment was done, and we left the hospital.

While on that same mission trip, I was asked to pray for a man who had not gotten up out of bed for twenty years. He was semi-comatose. He was bathed with a water hose and slept on a block of cement made into a bed. I was a little nervous because that was my first mission trip. I didn't feel experienced enough to pray for such a condition. I approached the bed and began to talk with him. I remembered my nursing training which taught hearing is the last sense to leave the body. I sat on the edge of that cement bed and told him what I was doing and who I was. I really didn't know what to do, so I think I was just prolonging the time until the Lord moved me. Then, it happened. God reminded me of the story of Tabitha in Acts 9. Tabitha was told to "arise." The Holy Spirit whispered, "Tell this man to arise."

Because I was a new missionary, I felt insecure acting upon what only I heard: to tell a semi-comatose man to arise. However, I was obedient to the still small voice.

"In the name of Jesus Christ of Nazareth," I told the man, "I command you to arise and be healed." Within moments, the man was awake. We took him outside to bathe him under the hose, and I went to buy clothes for him because he had lain there naked for years. That evening, we took him to a gathering, and he ate with all of us. He and I walked down the village paths together toward the large lake. It was a surreal experience. It felt like I was walking in the villages where Jesus walked, and the lake we approached seemed like the Sea of Galilee. His neighbors and everyone were utterly amazed.

On a mission trip to Goma, Kenya, a group of pastors were meeting at the mud hut of another pastor woman. She was no ordinary pastor woman. She had no education, nor could she read or write, but she had started three churches and walked thirty miles every Sunday to get to them.

When we met, I turned my attention to a small child lying on the mat. I noticed he had not moved and was breathing heavily as if gasping for air. I recognized the Cheyne-Stokes breathing pattern from my days of nursing. I approached the child, and the mother told me the child had been very ill.

"Oh no, devil!" I declared, "In the name of Jesus Christ of Nazareth, be healed and get up from this death bed." That night, the child was running and playing with all the other children in the village. The child is still alive today.

Missionaries stand firm when they face many dangers. High-risk situations exist everywhere. Weather conditions, diseases, accidents, theft, bandits, pirates, and roadside robbers are just a few of the real possibilities. Many of these were not just possibilities for me.

Roaches and Bandits

The heat in Goma, Kenya was intense. The average daily temperature could be over 120 degrees. I slept inside a mud hut where the mud retained heat, and the mosquito net that I slept under added at least ten degrees more. That was an impossible situation for me. The heat of the kitchen added even more heat to the mud hut, which had little ventilation. The bed mattress was made of clothes, and there was no such thing as a pillow at that time. My head was near a cardboard box sitting on top of other boxes. Whatever was inside it caused thousands of huge roaches to squirm around making horrible creeping noises. I might have been able to deal with that. However, I flicked on my flashlight to go outside to the toilet—that means squatting on the ground! At my head was a long line of huge roaches going back and forth on the headboard just five inches away from me. It was impossible to keep them out, for the hut was made of mud and has many open spaces. It is not an enclosed home like westerners are used to. That did it; I went outside to sleep under the open sky on a mat. At that time, I wasn't aware of the dangers of scorpions or the strong night winds blowing in my face. Neither was I aware of the possibility of bandits coming to rob me.

I was outside with the children singing and telling Bible stories until at least midnight. One of the village young men came home and announced that there were four men on the way to our hut. He said he had passed them on the way home, and they were less than a quarter mile away. They had AK-47s and were saying they were coming to rob the "*mzungu*" at Bishop's hut. Mzungu means "white person" in Swahili. In many nations, being white implies you are rich. It means you have money and valuable goods to give away. Therefore, even if someone takes things from you without your permission, it is not considered stealing because you have those things to give.

The young man told Bishop. Immediately, Bishop went to the consular's hut to try to find another hut for me to spend the night. The consular holds a political office. While he scurried there, I was left with the children. I remembered Jehoshaphat in 2 Chronicles 20:22,

> *"And when they began to sing and to praise, the LORD set ambushments against the children of Ammon, Moab, and mount Seir, which were come against Judah; and they were smitten."*

I told the children about this verse and had half of them went to one side of the hut to sing, and the other half went to the other side to sing. I knew the bandits had no chance then. I went in the back of the hut and prayed. I lifted my finger up to heaven.

"God, you brought me here. Now, you protect me," I said. "Now, you make all of those who are my intercessors in America wake up and pray for me now. "

I should not have been surprised later, but I was. I returned home to America the following week, and I was greeted by my friend.

"What happened to you last week?" she asked. "God woke me up and told me to pray for your protection." All I could do was laugh. God is so awesome and faithful.

As the chldren sang, Bishop returned and quickly took me to the consular's hut. They wanted to place me by myself inside in the hut in order to give me the best they had. I was too nervous to be alone, so I slept outside on a mat with the family. We all lined up, each on his or her mat, in single file. The father was at the first end, and the mother was at the other end to protect their young, who were in the middle. I was also in the middle. The consular had his AK-47 by his side. I fell off to sleep only to be awakened at five in the morning with a screaming rooster running across my chest. That will get your attention and wake you up quickly!

The father did what most African Christian fathers do: he began to pray for his family as they woke up and to give thanks to God for another day of life.

It wasn't long after I arrived home that I received the word. The leader of that bandit group became paralyzed. I never wished the group any harm. I never prayed for revenge on them. But God does not take it lightly when you mess with one of His own. 1 Chronicles 16:22 says, *"Touch not mine anointed, and do my prophets no harm."*

Rain and Roadside Pirates

Bishop, his wife, and I were on our way to Nairobi. I was leaving Kenya after being there almost two months. I wanted to get to Nairobi a couple of days early to be sure I would get to the airport on time because the trip was always hard and unpredictable. We travelled in a bus on the desert sand, which was the only road out of Goma. It was a two-day drive, which required an overnight stay in the middle of the trip. That night in the local hotel, the Lord told me to read a verse in Haggai. That woke me up!

Haggai 1:8, *"Go up to the mountain, and bring wood, and build the house; and I will take pleasure in it, and I will be glorified, saith the LORD."*

The Lord impressed upon me to go to the mountain. I didn't know a mountain. I was on my way to Nairobi.

It was only three in the morning, and I couldn't sleep again. I impatiently waited until the daylight. As soon as I saw it, I knocked on Bishop and his wife's door.

"Bishop, get up. The Lord told me to go to the mountain. I don't know a mountain."

Immediately, he said, "I do." It was as if God had spoken to him also.

Bishop called someone and made an appointment to meet us upon arrival. We boarded the matatu (minibus) with fifteen people squashed into the small vehicle. I insisted on sitting in the front seat. I get a bit claustrophobic, and the smells that assault my senses when I ride in the back of a matatu (minibus) nauseate me. I also feel a sense of panic, wondering how I would get out if we had an accident. Usually, Bishop had to negotiate a seat for me in the front. If it upset people, we would just wait for the next matatu. That could be hours, but God made a way for us on the trip. I was the first to pay and choose my seat up front.

We headed on our "safari." The word "safari" means journey, but we Westerners are used to hearing it refer to a trip to see the animals on the reserves.

The trip went smoothly until night came. As we drove up the mountain, the heavy rains began. The night was pitch black with no roadside lamps. The driver was struggling to keep the matatu on the narrow, slippery clay road. We were slipping and sliding. I saw it all through the windshield. I just kept calm and prayed. No one said a word; then, we stopped.

Why did we stop? I wondered. I couldn't see anything. Then, two men came out of the bush. Then, I could see. They had placed a huge tree across the road. They were pirates, and they intended to rob us. The driver got out of the matatu. I began to sing and pray. Now you don't know like I know, but the key I sang in wasn't even on the keyboard. I couldn't help myself. The Spirit of God overtook me, and I sang out loud. I felt sorry for those poor people who had to listen, but no one told me to be quiet. Most of them were Christians, and they too were praying. After some words, money was exchanged, and the driver got back in the vehicle. The pirates moved the tree, and we continued our trip slip-sliding away. No one said a word.

We arrived several hours later into the early morning. We got a hotel. What was the cost? Shofar Sound had to pay five dollars! Yes, you can imagine, a five-dollar-a-night hotel room. God provided. I have stayed in worse with roaches crawling all over my mosquito net and up the walls. Our host met us, and I couldn't wait to see why God sent us there.

The next day was Sunday, and I was asked to preach. It was a very powerful meeting. People were saved and delivered, but it was not anything different than my usual experience. As the day began to close, I asked the Lord if that meeting was the only reason He brought me there. Soon after that, we were invited to dinner and to go pray for a family.

The rain was still very hard, and the skies were dark again.

We walked for about two miles, and all of us, except Bishop and a pastor, entered the house. They stayed outside to discuss some issues. All I knew about the family was they had converted to Christianity from Islam; all had received Christ as their personal Savior. I was told they were experiencing great warfare.

As soon as I entered the home, I felt a group of demons push against me. It felt heavy, and I couldn't breathe. I immediately had to run outside and call for Bishop. I told him we needed to pray *right then,* not after dinner. I told him to please come inside and begin praying with us. He heard the urgency and the spirit of my voice and came right in. Thank God for my ability to discern spirits and to not be afraid of those in the unseen world. The Bible says in Romans 8:37, *"Nay, in all these things we are more than conquerors through him that loved us."*

That is when I understood why we had so many problems getting there in that matatu and why I sang publicly when I can't carry a tune. Still, I didn't know everything yet. I took the lead as the Holy Spirit led me. I asked the father of the home what was happening. He described how the family would all get sick at the same time, how they would all not be able to breathe at the same time, and how something would be on the table and just a minute later it would be missing. He told many stories relating to the phenomenon.

As I listened to the Holy Spirit, I was led to ask who in the home had sinned. At first no one admitted to the indiscretion, but soon after, the mother left to do something in another room, and the pastors and I were left alone with the father. That's when he admitted he had sinned. I didn't ask him what sin. I just explained that God protects His people but sin allows the enemy access. The local pastor explained that the Imam from the local Mosque prays for evil spirits to harass those who have left the Islamic faith. We are protected from those evil spirits, but sin gives them permission to torment and have entrance into our lives.

I asked the father to gather the family and asked him if he would be willing to ask for forgiveness from God. He agreed and did so; then, he led his entire family to repent for their sins. The bishop and his wife, the two pastors, and I began to move in the Spirit and cast out the demons from the home; we then laid hands on each of the family members. We prayed for quite some time until we felt the spirits leave and the peace of God fill the house. Every family member was slain in the Spirit of God and laid out on the floor under the power of the Holy Spirit. Even the three-year-old awakened and said in Swahili, "I can breathe now. I feel peace." We ate a great meal of ugali and beef rejoicing over what God had done, and in the morning, we headed for Nairobi and had an uneventful ride.

We never know what God has planned. Our job is to be obedient and available. I was in the Philippines when asked to go and pray for a couple with two children. The couple believed their children had been cursed. I was in Mindanao, and the place was under the mountain where I was told was very near to the New People's Army (NPA), the guerilla arm of the communist party of the Philippines. Two of the other team members who came with me on the mission trip refused to go into that area. They stayed behind and hid inside the local police hut.

I was taken ahead on a motorcycle. The others would follow later. I rode the motorcycle about five miles into the foothills, where I was dropped off at a nipa bamboo hut. Inside the hut were a man and woman who couldn't speak English. However, I didn't want to waste any time because I was aware of the dangers around me. I thought it best to go ahead and begin to pray. My prayer was strong, and the anointing came over me. I blessed the mother and father, blessed the hut, the land, and all that was around me. The parents began to cry together and hug each other like they were falling in love all over again.

I had no idea I was at the wrong hut. The motorcycle driver wanted to protect me until some others in my group were there, but God knew, and He had planned to use me somehow in that hut as well. The man and wife later told the group how I had blessed them and how they needed that prayer.

Finally, I was reunited to the group, and we went to the correct hut. We all prayed over the couple and their two children. God then gave me a message for them. He said the children were not cursed but were special, and He had specifically chosen their parents. God said those parents were chosen because they could be trusted to bring up the children and do the right thing. He said they were strong enough to deal with special children and He had already given them everything they needed to carry out their assignment. There was a time of rejoicing; then, my motorcycle carried me out to where I could join the ones who were afraid to enter.

Broken Down in Enemy Territory

The road to Goma from Nairobi was a two-day drive. We slept at the halfway mark where the bus stopped for the night. For the next ten hours, we drove through enemy territory. The sandy desert was riddled with large potholes and open ditches, which made the trip extremely challenging. So much sand and dust filled the vehicle that it even got inside the luggage. There were no exits, no toilets, and no restaurants, only the desert and us. Most of the vehicles were not kept up properly, so they had frequent breakdowns. The heat was unbearable. No air conditioner was available. AAA did not exist there. If the vehicle ran hot or had a flat tire, no service stations were available to assist you. You were on your own to figure out a plan.

As if that were not bad enough, everyone who travelled on that road had to go through the Baringo tribal territory. The Baringo and the Nilotic had been in tribal conflict for ages. Both tribes were pastoralist, and they both stole goats, sheep, camels, and other animals from the other. Stealing was only part of the problem. They would literally kill for the animals. One day as Bishop and I passed through, finally safe onto Nilotic land, we came across one local woman dressed in layer after layer of beads around her neck and a sheet around her body. She was walking toward the thirty-mile journey to Goma. Bishop asked if we could pick her up and give her a lift. It was common for those who have a vehicle to try to ease the burden of those who don't. When we made introductions, Bishop talked to her about her family. The Baringo tribe had recently killed her husband when they stole his animals.

Herding animals was the livelihood of both tribes. They sold the animals for money, food, skins, clothing, and milk. The tribes were wanderers or nomads. They could be found wandering from place to place in search of water for their animals. If you read the

Bible stories of Abraham and Jacob, you could imagine the terrain and the lifestyle of those tribes. It reminds me of that every time I go. It seems little has changed since Biblical times.

When I first started going to Goma, there was no airport, so a small plane was out of the question. I usually took the bus, along with the goats and chickens, to Goma. Now, small planes fly daily in and out of Goma to Nairobi. However, flying is very expensive, especially when you were required to pay for all of those travelling with you.

The first time I went to Goma, I hired a vehicle. No, I didn't go up to an Enterprise, Budget, or Dollar Rent a Car and ask for one. I went to the streets of Nairobi. Bishop and I looked about; then, Bishop negotiated with someone who owned a for-hire vehicle. Bishop usually goes and negotiates and then returns to tell me the cost because when they see the mzungu, the price triples. The owner gets upset when I finally get into the car, and he realizes what happened.

On the first trip, it was important that I see the area, and I wanted a little more control of the stops because I had not experienced what was ahead. I needed more control over bathroom breaks and which bush I wanted to use.

The driver wanted to have one of his buddies go with us to help him drive. Bishop and I refused because to have two of them increased the dangers of being robbed and killed. Twenty minutes into the drive, the driver received a phone call. He was told that I left some luggage and needed to return. Bishop and I were smarter than that. We pulled out the luggage and checked it. I had not left anything. It was a trick to get us to return for some reason: perhaps to rob me, to charge me more, or to force someone in the car with us. We told the driver to keep driving and not to answer his phone any more.

Another time Bishop, another pastor, and I needed to leave Goma and go to a distant village. It would take at least ten hours. I hired a vehicle and driver from Goma. A pastor I knew got the vehicle for us, so I was confident it was okay. On the way, the driver decided to pass on a side road where the sand had not been well packed. We got stuck right in enemy territory. Our SUV was deep into the sand. Two children were sitting on a rock in the desert and came to help us. It seemed they sat there just for that reason, so they could make a few shillings at the end of the day. Our vehicle, however, was stuck too deeply. We had nothing to help us. The more we dug the sand and put tree limbs under it to get leverage, the deeper we sank.

For six hours, we were stranded in the fierce heat—in the Baringo territory, no less. Soon, the night animals would be out. I'd seen hyenas and the leftovers of elephants in the area. Snakes and other dangerous animals would possibly be our guests for the night. I had no place to sit, except on a tree trunk or on the sand. Mostly, I just walked in circles praying for our safety. It was almost nightfall and from the road someone, who had the proper equipment to pull us out, saw us.

Praise the Lord! That vehicle got us to our destination without another incident, but on the way back, it was a different story. We broke down five times and ran out of gas (the gas gauge didn't work). The fifth time we broke down, we were only three hours outside of Goma. So, we called someone to come and get us. We sat in the heat by the side of the road until they arrived. God's hand of protection is over His servants. Although there are many troubles, trials, and tribulations, the Bible says the Lord delivers us from all of them (Psalms 34:19).

Mission Is: Giving

Another characteristic of mission is giving. God calls each of us to fill in the gap, so the Word of God can be spread throughout the world. Mission contributes to the spiritual and the natural hunger of mankind. In order to feed people spiritually, their stomachs must be fed naturally. A missionary feeds the body and nourishes the spirit. Not only does the missionary need to give, but someone must give to the mission and the missionary.

A political and tribal conflict broke out in Kenya during a presidential campaign, creating the need for internally displaced people (IDP) camps. People, who had moved from their local areas to the larger city and built businesses and homes for their families, found themselves back in their tribal lands without food, water, and shelter. Tens of

> *Mission contributes to the spiritual and the natural hunger of mankind.*

thousands of men, women, and children were devastated from the conflict. Many had lost children, and some children were orphaned, looking for someone to care for them. I visited a few of those camps in Goma. While at one of these camps, I was asked to pray with people and speak to the church inside the camp.

As I was praying, I saw a vision. I saw five hundred people gathered around the church, and Shofar Sound was feeding them.

Then, I saw a worship service that went until midnight under the stars. I spoke to Bishop and asked how possible it was to bring the vision to pass. Bishop called the pastors of the eighteen churches in the camp for all to come together. We met that night in order to plan. Early the next morning, we set out to buy several goats and ugali flour. Pastors called for their churches to come together, and the same evening we had singing, praying, and various pastors speaking to over five hundred people. We worshipped under the moon and stars of the open African sky.

All too frequently we saw people starving because of lack of food and money. In Goma, food was scarce and had to be brought in from Kitale and Nairobi. After the hard trip on top of buses in the extreme heat, much of the fresh fruits and vegetables were withered and barely fit for consumption. Fish that was caught in Lake Nilotic, three hours away, was dried in the open air. When I visited Lake Nilotic, the orphan children caught the fish with their hands and sometimes with a spear. They laid the fish out on a mat, and at the end of the day it was cooked by the sun. They tore the fish with their teeth as I watched them enjoy their meal.

Animals experienced starvation as well. Rib cages highlighted the structure of the animals. Poverty, drought, and hunger plagued many of the places I had been called to preach. How could I preach when stomachs were so empty?

Digging the Well

All too often, basic necessities of life, such as water, are not available to villagers in many third world countries. In Goma, water was scarce. Many walked miles in search of water. Seeing this, I wondered what I could do. I was just one woman and didn't think I could do anything by myself, but with God all things are possible.

I was shopping in the Navy Exchange one day when the telephone rang. At our first meeting months before, I told Adelaide about Shofar Sound and the work we do. I told her about the conditions of Goma. Little did I know what she had been doing since our meeting.

"Chara," I heard over the phone, "this is Adelaide. I don't know what I would do if I didn't have water. So, I have been sewing and selling my shoe bags. I have collected $1000 as seed money for you to dig a well in Goma."

"DIG A WELL!" I didn't know the first thing about wells. As a child, we had a pump, and I knew how to pump the water, but not dig one? I was trapped, cornered. I was set up for something God wanted to accomplish, so He had chosen some simple things (me and a lady making shoe bags) of the world to confound the wise. Adelaide had designated money specifically for the project, and I had to make it happen. But how? By faith and I mean *by faith*! So, I wrote an appeal letter to ask for funds to dig a well in Goma. People began to give. I was in deeper kimchi then.

I had many sleepless nights. I was only one woman, and I couldn't remember anything in my past that prepared me for that mission. Well maybe, courage, determination, integrity, common sense, and project management skills counted. That was all I had. When I thought about a retired, military, female nurse going to the arid desert of Africa to dig a well, it just blew my mind.

I searched the Internet and called people with knowledge of

digging wells. The more I learned, the more complicated it seemed to get. I learned about shallow wells, deep wells, rigs and all sorts of things, like dowsing, that I had never heard about. I was at panic stage. I had asked people in Goma for information, but that proved useless. Maybe they knew the impossibilities of a single woman coming to oversee a well project. Maybe they just thought it would never happen. My donors asked me specific questions, and I tried to answer intelligently, but truthfully I knew very little. Only God was guiding me.

Bishop found the names of three well drillers in the area who gave cost quotes. Months later, money collected from trusting donors, I boarded the plane and headed for Goma, still having no great insight as to how it would get accomplished.

I may not have had knowledge about digging a well, but I had good business sense. I knew how to pray and how to trust God. Bishop and I met with several people and formed a team to interview the well drillers and make a contract. We discussed our strategies and then met with the contractors. We detailed the elements of the contract, and the contract was signed. I didn't sign the contract, nor did I put it in Shofar Sound's name, just in case there was a legal issue that would keep me bound for a long time in the country. Besides, the well was not going to be mine; it was for the people of the Togo Village just outside of Goma. I placed the contract in the name of Bishop's church. I just made a statement on the contract that it was a vision of Shofar Sound Ministries, Int'l. I called for the village chief to join us and place his official stamp on the contract. That required putting a little money under the table for him. That is the way business is done in the third world.

We really were going to dig a well for the Togo Village!

The first step was to determine a likely place that water could be reached. The driller considered the way the rivers flowed and the distance of the closest river. He considered where outdoor toilets were, so we wouldn't get the water where urine and feces had penetrated the ground. I learned a lot.

Then, it was time for me to teach them. I said we must pray over the site. We marched seven times around the sight that we had circled off with string. Seven is God's perfect number and means completion. Each time we marched, we quoted our version of Numbers 21:17, *"Spring up oh well, the Lord will give us water."* That became our theme song for drilling. The contractors sang it every day, all day long as they drilled. The verse and idea came from one of the donors, an elderly man who was very sick and wanted to donate $500. He gave all he had, but he was so happy to give. Now, a well thrives, in large part because of Adelaide, that gentleman, and others.

Building the School

I thought digging a well was a quite an ordeal. It certainly was the most challenging experience on the mission field that I had to that point. I had built a toilet and shower house, but that was nothing compared to digging a well. It was done, and I was sure I was through. I had accomplished the big thing God wanted done. I thought there could be no more challenges like that. Little did I know God had just given me a "precursor" project. God had given me a smaller thing to prepare me for the larger one He had in mind. God keeps training you.

Bishop happened to mention he wanted to start a school for adults. Most of the adults in his village were illiterate, but the 21st Century was slowly entering their lives. Education would be their key to joining the modern world. Bishop had researched the possibility with the government and had certified teachers willing to teach. He showed me the business plan. I had just built a well, and I thought I was done. I mean "well" done!

When I returned to the USA, the Lord kept nagging me about the school. I tried to ignore the call, but I knew better. The toilet was a $1500 project, the well was a $6000 project, and the school would be at least $15,000. What was God doing? Each time, the projects got bigger and more stressful. How could I raise that kind of money? I was just one woman and a small organization.

I determined I would build a foundation with walls and roof. That would suffice as a school and would certainly be less stress for me. I asked an architect to design a building as I described, so I could have a picture of the idea. By faith, I wrote letters and called people asking for donations. People were very excited about the school and willing to give for such a good cause. I had raised enough money for travel and expenses; however, I still needed $15,000 for the school. It was just a few weeks away from the departure time. My gift of faith and praying was all I had to work with.

One day, my brother called and asked if I had gone to the post office yet. What? He hardly ever called, and what a silly question to ask me? I told him I was out of town, but I was on my way home. He called again and asked me the same question.

It was too late; the post office was closed when I got home. I was curious by then, so I rose early and made it to the post office as soon as it opened. A letter had come from someone I had not seen or heard from in years, except on Facebook. I opened the letter with curiosity, and to my amazement, there was a check for $15,000. Was it real? How did my brother know? The person had won the lottery and donated to both my brother's ministry and mine.

I was just weeks away from leaving when God provided for the project. He always made me wait until the last minute. I guess that was so I could trust Him more. I wondered if I learned to not worry and fret if I would get the money any sooner. Hmm. I should try it. I know God's timing is always perfect timing.

On the ground in Goma, we formed a group to oversee the contract signing. The village chief joined us. We agreed to pay the contractor in three stages and defined them clearly. I was surprised when the contractor showed me in detail how he would build the school and would make sure it was done according to government standards. All of the worrying I had done proved to be for nothing. He described a 9 X 12 building, with an additional space for a teacher's conference room. He added two toilets: one for male and one for female. It was all for the same price I had negotiated.

Construction began on the building. Building the school seemed like the most difficult thing I had to ever been involved with in my life. The contractor did well until the end of the project. It was Christmas time, the school was almost completed, and the contractor left the project. Many of the workers said he went on a drinking binge. All I knew for sure was that he didn't return, and I was left with twenty-four African men in Bishop's yard asking for me. They were angry because they had not been paid. They were getting paid daily and up until that point, they had been paid. Because I hired the contractor, I paid the contractor, and it was his responsibility to pay the workers. They needed to go after him, but Africans didn't see it that way. They came after the mzungu.

Bishop and I called the village chief, and I had to give him some money under the table. He found the contractor, and after many hours of negotiations, the contractor came back on the scene and paid the workers. It sounds so simple as I write it and summarize it into one little paragraph. If you only knew the days of pain and anguish I went through—not to mention the fear of twenty-four angry African men staring you in the face. Nevertheless, the project was finally complete. The sign was painted, and Shofar Sound School was built.

The adult school provides a two-year program that allows adults to get their high school diploma. For many reasons, these adults did not have the opportunity to finish and now in modern times, they were having hard times finding a job. Herding animals was no longer a profitable occupation. The 21st Century required more eduction and better skills. The Shofar Sound School could help adults obtain those 21st Century needs.

The school is still in operation and has graduated over two hundred and forty students to date. Many of those students have gone on to get certificates in teaching and accounting. Some are working in county offices, and others have become village chiefs. We still desperately need another classroom, a science laboratory, and computer laboratory because the school is so popular. At least, we have made a great start.

God Provides

It is important for the missionary to give, but that can only happen when others give to the missionary. God has called all of us to participate in mission work. For some, that means to go to the field, and for others that means to support those who go. When you give towards mission work, God rewards you beyond your imagination.

I was just a few hours away from boarding my flight to Kenya. I still needed $500. I didn't even worry about it. I merely prayed softly in tongues all day, as I packed. I was about to close my computer when I saw an email that said, "You have money from PayPal."

What was PayPal? I had not heard of it yet. I thought it might be a scam, but I proceeded to open the email, and it said a man had donated $500 to Shofar Sound. I was absolutely astounded. It was just the amount I was asking for, and just hours before I was due to leave, God sent it. I called the man and told him the story. He said, "I'm glad you didn't ask for $1000."

God is a provider and is ever faithful. I know that man was blessed for obeying God's voice.

There is Grace in the Calling

The word "grace" means favor. Grace is the unmerited favor of God. When you are in agreement with God and His plan for your life, you walk in special favor. His Divine strength and help enables you to endure the impossible and the unthinkable.

The grace of God is enormously tangible when I am on the mission field. His presence overtakes me, and I am able to do things I would never dream of doing. It seems as if He told me to walk through a wall, I would be able to do so. My gift of faith kicks in at a supernatural level.

When I return home, I am amazed by the events, and often, I just spend time in tears weeping in humility and awe.

When you are called and you are walking in that call, there is a special anointing or grace that accompanies you that is not present with just anyone. When you walk in that calling, you can be assured God is with you and will never forsake you.

8

How Do You Know You Have Been Called?

Questions

As I near the close of this book, I wonder if you have questions about your calling.

+ How do you know you've been called?
+ How do you prepare? How do you know it is time?
+ How do you stay plugged in to be elevated even more?
+ How do you avoid detours and traps while moving in your calling?
+ How do you avoid people wanting to raise you up?
+ Are you worried about lack of funds to do what God has called you to do?

Do you know the answer to these questions?

Answering the Primary Call

How do you know you have been called? This is one of the most important questions you can ask. It is essential to know you have a call on your life and that you have a desire to fulfill it. First and foremost is to recognize and respond to your primary call. This is the call to come and enter into the family of God. This is the call to receive the redemption through His grace and mercy. Before you can walk in your destiny, you must answer the primary call of grace. This calling is for everyone. You don't have to hear a voice or see a sign. You simply agree with God that He sent Jesus to redeem the world, that Jesus is God Himself, and that He has a plan and purpose for your life. To agree with God is simply to say a prayer from your heart. The prayer tells God you repent or turn away from your sins and turn to God. Asking forgiveness is telling God you are sorry for sinning against Him and inviting Him to live within you. He lives in you by the Holy Spirit. This is the One who dwells inside of you, leads, guides, and instructs you.

Before you can walk in your destiny, you must answer the primary call of grace.

Some try to minimize Him, by calling Him an "it," or your consciousness, or your inner self. I like to call Him by who He is. He is the Holy Spirit living and dwelling within you when you acknowledge and accept Christ as Lord and Savior of all. You can receive your primary calling only by God's grace through faith (Ephesians 2:8). Nothing else can help you. No amount of work can bring you to your primary call. The Bible teaches that we will be judged according to our works (Romans 2:6). We cannot be "saved" by our works, but we will be judged by our works. Salvation is a free gift from God simply because of His death and resurrection. Salvation is given to all those who merely believe Jesus is Lord and then by asking Him to come into your heart.

However, after that, you will be excited and made so alive you will not be able to contain yourself. You will have an overwhelming desire to fulfill the work Jesus has called you to do. Your destiny will cry out from within, and the seed inside you will be activated. You will *want* to work for the Lord.

Identifying the Secondary Call

God will guide you to fulfill His purpose in you. Philippians 1:6 assures us of that. God began a good work in you, and God will complete that work in you. Have you noticed a longing or yearning inside of you to do something? What is that something? What has God showed you? What is your dream? What is your passion? There are no standardized 1-2-3 steps to identifying your calling. However, there *are* certain spiritual disciplines that draw you closer to God, so you can hear and understand His will for your life. God will make your calling clear. He most often confirms it in the Word of God. Listen to the still small voice. He will not let you miss your calling.

Tools to Identify the Secondary Calling

Saturate and Meditate

To help you identify your calling, you want to drench your heart and mind with the Word of God. Saturate and mediate. This fills you with truth and strength. It makes hearing God easier. You are reading God's living Word, and it speaks.

Now you want to pray, fast, and listen. Prayer is a two-way communication with God. You speak, and He listens. Some people stop there, but you need to keep going. Let God speak while *you* listen. Sit or lie quietly before the Lord. You won't always hear a voice, but watch carefully. Observe and discern the various things you see spiritually that you didn't see before. Listen with your spiritual and natural ear. Listen. What is God saying? Watch. What is God doing?

Fast

Fasting is giving up something, usually food, in order to seek God in certain matters. In one way, it says, "I'm starving for you, Lord." Set a specific time frame to fast. This can be one meal, one day, three days, seven days, or more. Determine what it is you will give up. Will you give up just meat or all food? Will you eat only vegetables and no starch or meat? Determine exactly what you will do and for how long. Determine what it is you are asking of God. Sometimes, you can fast just to be nearer to Him. You don't have to ask for anything, except a closer walk with Him. During a fast, you should abstain from television, telephone, or other distractions as much as possible. It is a time of consecration to God. God is the center of your focus. You are actually empting out yourself to God and filling yourself with His Word. Listen to godly music, pray, read the Bible, and lay quietly, listening and meditating on Him and who He is. Fasting sharpens your spiritual ears and eyes. It is a powerful spiritual discipline.

Identify Your Gifts

Knowing who you are and what gifts you have helps you to realize your calling. Identify what gifts you have by writing them down. Be patient, specific, and lengthy. List everything you can think of.

You can also make a list of who you are. Write as many characteristics about yourself and your character, your personality, your strengths, and your weaknesses (see the following example). Meditate over these lists. What similarities and differences do you see? What patterns can you identify? What is God saying in your life? Ask God to show you what all this means and to direct your path. He will help you to know yourself and your gifts.

Knowing who you are and what gifts you have helps you to realize your calling.

To further your endeavor, you may want to spend time thinking about the needs of the world. What is wrong and what is right with the world, your country, your state, and other entities that may have significance to you? What of those things moves your heart? Where do you sense a strong burden? Is it in the current refugee crisis, abortion issues, racial discrimination, people who are sick, child molestation, drug issues, politics, rape victims, or people who are hurt? Where and how do you see yourself being able to use your gifts? Try to define very specifically who you are and how you function? For example, I knew I get bored after I learn a job. I don't like to stay in one area for more than three or four years. This is probably a result of growing up in a pastor's home where the organization moved the pastor about every three to five years. I knew being a forty-year loyal employee doing the same job for a company would definitely not work for me. However, I like stability of working with the same entity. The military afforded me the opportunity of moving often but still being with the same "company." That was perfect for me.

Pray and seek God's leading. Ask Him to reveal your intricate nature. It is important to have strong spiritual leaders you can talk to. Discuss your thoughts and ideas with someone you can trust. Spiritual leaders help to confirm what you see and hear. They also help to stimulate other ideas and opportunities you might not see. They are able to see you in a different way than you see yourself. They are able to ask many thought provoking questions to help you think outside of the box and really dig deep into yourself.

It is also important to be patient. Remember, God works in His time and not yours. You may be called and see your calling clearly, but it is in God's timing that it will be fulfilled. Being still is sometimes the hardest part of walking in your calling. It is a time when you may begin to question God or His call on your life. It is a time when discouragement can enter in, and the devil uses this to try and defeat you. Discouragement is one of the devil's main weapons. In times of waiting on God, you must remember to stay connected, keep praying, stay in the Word, fast, and praise and worship Him.

Organize the List

After you have a long list, then you can categorize the list. Organize the gifts that have an affinity (likeness) to each other; then, title each category. This process will help you consolidate and systematize a long list into their natural relationships. You will hopefully be able to generate insights about your destiny by using the diagram. See the simple example on the next page.

TEACHING	ORGANIZING	MISSIONARY	GIFTS
Passion for teaching	Natural ability to immediately observe disorder and imagine how it can be organized into order	Work well with others from many ethnic groups	Gift of tongues
People respond well when I teach.	Love order and structure	Have strong perseverance and determination	Gift of discernment
Enjoy learning, researching, and going to school	Experience in organizing data into information	Have great insight	Gift of Prophesy
Education (BS in Nursing, Master's in Management, Theology, Cross Cultural Studies), DMin	Experience in organizing people's homes, garages	Enjoy helping people through difficult situations	When I lay hands and pray with people, often demons come out and many get healed.
Able to take complicated concepts and break them down into easy to understand outlines	Experience in organizing infrastructure of hospital committees and departments	Love to travel	Many people call me to pray for them.
Ability to capture and keep one's attention for long period of time	Good at organizing information into charts and graphs	Adventurous – love trying new things, all kinds of new foods, even dangerous places	Enjoy praying for people and seeing them receive breakthrough
Ability to plan and organize		Love diversity	People respond to God when I preach
Confident		Love understanding cultures	Military background- able to understand spiritual warfare and strategies
Many computer skills		Gift of faith	Can see and understand when others don't
Ability to influence		Love remote and primitive environments	
Possess the gift of gab		Able to be content having or not having	
		Can work hard for many hours	
		Nursing skills and experience	

Mapping Your Life

I've learned that one possible strategy to help identify your gifts and destiny is to map your life.

Documenting major events of your past helps you to see your future. Write out events of your life and then place them in chronological order. Identify feelings, emotions, challenges, and successes associated with each event. Connect as many situations as possible to places, times, and others involved. You may want to categorize the events and list similar events under the same category. Study and contemplate the chart you have created. Ponder your map over several sessions, so you can *listen* to your life. Ask questions. Have you become stuck in a certain pattern? What excites you? What drains you? What is connected to a dream or a gifting? What negative things, such as a divorce, can be used for helping others now that you have conquered them? Is there a certain group you seem to care about or a target population that may seem common in your life? You may see that you are drawn to the poor or to those who have been neglected, sexually abused, or in prison. Mapping your life will help you readily identify patterns, desires, passions, dreams, and dislikes. This process provides a framework, which gives insight and clarity, not only about your past, but also about your future. It helps you to see the burdens you have for others and identifies some significant events that led you to this concern. It helps to identify any hindrances and limitations to fulfill your calling.

The map will help you see patterns and directions in your life. Get creative with your mapping chart. Look at samples on the Internet to get ideas as well. I am merely providing a list of suggestions to demonstrate what types of events might go into a map. With each event, you will want to describe your feelings, thoughts, and circumstances. The purpose is for you can look back on your life and identify patterns of where you have been and how you might have arrived at your current place in life. You will also see patterns that will help you to determine possible opportunities for the future.

A <u>simple and incomplete example</u> map may be something like this.

- Born to parents who love and serve the Lord Jesus. Dad is a pastor. Mom is a great helpmate, organizer, and singer. I could follow by example.
- Dad always wanted to be in the military but was called to preach.
- Mom wanted to be a nurse, but her dad discouraged her, saying it was no life for a woman.
- Grew up in church. Provided a great foundation.
- Moved to many places in my childhood. Learned to be flexible and how to adapt.
- Began working (babysitting and cleaning homes) at an early age because I liked it.
- Driven by desire to work. Got job at Jack's Hamburgers at age 14 and nursing aid job at nursing home at 16, with worker's permit.
- Began driving at age 15.
- Littletown, Alabama School

- Littletown private school during racial integration issues in the south.
- High school 1974-77.
- Began nursing school at age 18; School of Nursing 1977-80 (Diploma).
- Worked in ICU/Open Heart Recovery- Medical Center and University.
- Joined military 1981.
- Married at age 18. Young and determined. No wisdom. Self-willed. Hardheaded. Rebellious. Led to major life event later.
- Joined United States Navy at age 20. Became Commander Nurse Corps. Retired 1998.
- Annulled marriage after fourteen years.
- Met another man. With him 12 years – not married. Moved to New Jersey, New York. Worked at AIDS facility. Worked at New York State appointed by Governor.
- Lost boyfriend and job Nov. 2002. Broken heart, depression, led to my spiritual awakening in Nov. 2002.
- Moved to California 2003
- Got the gift of tongues Feb. 2004
- Started seminary 2004-2006
- Mission trip 2005-Philippines
- Mission trips began 2005 in numerous places (Thailand, Uganda, Sudan, Egypt, Tanzania)
- Preaching in various ecumenical churches and events

- God used me to cast out demons – and healed many through me-Amazed
- Teacher of Bible- Seminars- Public speaking
- Doctorate of Mininstry— Higher Ground Theological Seminary

Write as many characteristics about you and your character, your personality, your strengths, and your weaknesses. Categorize them according to periods of time in your life. You may choose to make a timeline chart for each of the events or categories of events. Meditate over these lists. What similarities and differences do you see? What patterns can you identify? What is God saying in your life? Ask God to show you what all this means. Ask Him to direct your path. He will help you to know yourself and your gifts.

Preparation for the Future

Preparation for your calling requires patience. Preparation for your calling is a lifelong process. Every aspect of your life has significance for your purpose. God continually trains and equips those He calls. That does not mean you won't get to live out your dream until you are old. It does mean that even though you may be walking in your calling, you will continually be positioned or repositioned. Just when you think you have arrived, God will take you through an experience to test your character, to build strength, and to increase your faith. He will continue to grow you throughout your life in order to elevate you. Don't despise the character building or strengthening exercises. Remember Joseph when he finally arrived at Potiphar's house. He was placed in charge. What more could he have dreamed. He probably thought he had arrived to the level God had shown him in the dream. No, God still had more for him. God allowed a terrible and painful situation to come his way. If God didn't, Joseph would have remained comfortable and would never have gone any higher. Potiphar's house was not the ultimate calling on Joseph's life. He was still being prepared for greater callings.

The most important part of preparation is to stay in tune with God. Stay in His Word, stay in prayer and stay connected. Listen, be obedient, willing, and available. When you increase in your spiritual discipline, you give God permission to be in charge. You decrease, and He increases.

Preparation may include higher-level education. A call to ministry may include seminary. A call to nursing will include school, as will most other professional callings. Even a call to vocations will include education. Education takes time, patience, and hard work. You may get frustrated. You may wonder if you will ever finish. You may begin to doubt and even get sidetracked. Don't lose focus. Keep your eyes, heart, mind, and concentration on the goal.

Knowing The Time

God's timing is not our timing. He is always on time, but for us, it almost always seems late or inconvenient. Oftentimes, God's timing is the last minute. It seems He waits until the moment before chaos breaks out. Psalms 37 tells us to be still and wait patiently for Him. This is extremely difficult if you are walking in your own strength. The period of waiting may be long and torturous.

It takes faith and perseverance. Discouragement can creep in and grip you. Discouragement can cause you to lose your footing, and this is precisely what the devil wants. Trust that God will give you direction. Proverbs 3:5-6 reminds us to trust Him and not to lean on our understanding but rather acknowledge Him, and He will direct your path. The word acknowledge means "to know" in the Hebrew. I said before that *knowing* was the first step in preparation. You must know Him and must know He will take you through. You must trust Him and know He has a plan, and it is good. You must know the wait is well worth it. When God begins to move, you will *know*. Doors will begin to open, and all you will have to do is walk through them. "Walking in" is still a *by faith* move.

As I began to prepare for a Tanzania mission, I fell very sick. Some days, I could hardly get out of bed. That was not me at all. I was sick for a few months. So many other catastrophes were happening in my life as well. I knew God had told me to go to Tanzania, but how could I go as sick as I was? I kept focused on the Word, and I stayed in prayer. I knew God would help me, but it took a lot of faith.

When God says move, you move. It's time.

I kept confirming God had told me to go, so I would go. The devil could not stop me. My friends kept trying to discourage me by asking me if God really told me to go. They didn't have my faith because it wasn't their calling. Finally, a few days before I left for Tanzania, my body began to heal. I was still a little weak, but by the time I landed, God had healed me. I am telling you this to let you know that you will still have to step out *by faith* even when it is the right time.

When God says move, you move. It's time.

Author's Note

The purpose of this book is to help you realize that every aspect of your life helps you to identify your calling. I believe it also gives insight into the world of missions. We are in a day where technology has allowed this world to become much smaller, but there is still a great need for people to go out into the uttermost. They are needed to speak a word of encouragement, to help feed a body and a soul, and to fulfill God's great commission.

In our current day of worldwide conflicts and war torn countries, much of the uttermost has migrated into more developed countries. Today, in America, we can find uttermost situations.

My hope is that this book opens the understanding of pastors and laity concerning the life of a missionary, which is by no means an easy work. The preparation and the process may take months or years to fulfill. However, the presence of a missionary in a forgotten and even unknown world is life changing for everyone. It is my desire that this book will not only open your eyes but your heart to the plight of those who are living in the uttermost and those who serve them.

Acknowledgements

Thank you, Lord, for salvation. Thank you for your grace and mercy.

Thank you to my parents who taught me well. My mom went to Heaven in 2009, and my dad entered into Glory in 2016, while I was on mission in Kenya, Zambia, and Tanzania. I dedicate this effort to their honor and memory.

Thank you to my brothers.

Thank you to the donors, supporters, and those who helped to make my story possible, by sending me forth into the uttermost to perform the calling on my life.

Thank you to Andreas Symphony, a four-time author, cherished friend, and a great woman of faith, for helping me bring order to the thoughts on these pages. I appreciate her time, patience, and shared vision of this work so each person who reads it receives inspiration and knowledge in addition to an understanding of what God considers ministering to those in the uttermost.

Thank you to a beloved professor who contributed not only in writing the foreword but educated me about missions and the special insights into culture and language.

Thank you to an esteemed woman of God for contributing

to the foreword and for always encouraging me and being a dear sister in Christ.

Thank you to those who reviewed my work and made suggestions for its success.

Thank you to the various educational institutions I have attended, which have given me a solid education. Now, I can support others in obtaining an education.

Printed in the United States
By Bookmasters